THE CLUB

DAVID EDWARDS

Copyright 2024

All Rights Reserved

ISBN

Hardcover: 978-1-917116-87-9

THE PADUCAH SUN-DEMOCRAT	
DATE	**ARTICLE TITLE**
18/08/1925	Lakeview Country Club Will Close Membership List, 25th
21/10/1925	Lakeview Course In Paducah Promises To Be Finest In Kentucky
20/12/1925	Lakeview Country Club Contract List
2/3/1926	Lakeview's Course Good
31/08/1926	Spanish Style Club House Is On a Fine Site
31/08/1926	Nearly Score Of Firms Take Part In The Construction And Furnishing Of Lakeview Club
31/08/1926	Golf Course At Lakeview Destined To Finest First Test Of Golf In Kentucky
8/1/1927	Stewart To Head Lake View Club
8/1/1927	Paxton, Goodman On Lakeview Club Board
23/03/1932	In Bankruptcy
5/5/1933	Commissioner's Safe
8/5/1933	Commissioner Sales Lakeview Property
21/03/1934	Government Seizes Lakeview Country Club Site As Camp For Training Idle Youths
20/04/1934	County Granted New Hearing In Lake View Case
20/04/1934	Suit Involves Misuse Of Cash By Utterback
27/08/1934	Camp Roosevelt Paints Out Its Benefits
20/04/1941	450 Attend Opening Of Country Club
21/04/1941	Forest Hills Country Club Has Formal Opening Saturday Night
11/12/1944	Chester McGuire Buys Forest Hills Country Club
9/3/1945	Flood Waters

12/6/1950	Lakeview Property Sold To Wells Health For $29,000
2/7/1952	Guthrie Investment Purchases Former Country Club Site
21/10/1952	Southwood Country Club Meeting Set, Wednesday Night
19/12/1952	Sunday To Be The Day For Proposed New Club
4/2/1953	New Country Club Here Is Chartered
10/3/1953	300 At New Country Club Open House Sunday
24/03/1953	Southwood Reaches 200 Member Goal
9/4/1953	24-Year Country Club Lease Signed
23/04/1953	Southwood Golf Course Will Introduce Tiffine Bermuda To This Area
16/10/1953	Sues For $100,000
25/09/1955	Financial Troubles Close Country Club
22/10/1955	Southwood May Be Re-Opened
26/10/1955	Bryan Advises Truce
29/03/1956	New Country Club Will Be Opened Here on Sunday
1/4/1956	Rolling Hills Open Today
26/05/1956	Southwood Settles Lawsuit

ABOUT THE AUTHOR

David Edwards, a retired business owner and entrepreneur with deep roots in Paducah, Kentucky, has found a new place to call home in the vibrant and sunny community of The Villages, Florida. A versatile athlete, David lettered in three sports at Lone Oak High School in Paducah.

By the age of 22, he had learned the classic golf swing, honing his skills in 1976 under the guidance of Vince Genovese, a distinguished and recently retired professional at Paxton Park. David's passion for the game and the camaraderie of the country club scene only grew, culminating in his election to the board of Rolling Hills Country Club in 1987. This position allowed him to influence the direction of his club and contribute to its development and success.

It was during his tenure on the board that a new creative endeavor began to take shape in my mind. The concept of writing a novella started to form, combining his rich experiences, imagination, and the insights gained from his journey on the board. This concept, long nurtured in the recesses of his mind, finally came to fruition upon his retirement.

PREFACE

The impetus for writing this novella stemmed from my initial participation in a board meeting as a newly elected member. Although the individuals comprising the former board were individually decent, their collective mindset had evolved into a belief that only they possessed the ability to govern the club effectively. This perception seemingly originated when Paul Friedlander established an autocratic ruling class at the club's inception, purportedly due to the property owner's insistence that Paul retains absolute control in exchange for leasing the property.

At times throughout the book, you may perceive a hint of self-righteousness. Despite the fact that most of my ideas aligned with the majority of members' thoughts, I, as a board member, made mistakes. I opposed the sale of the property, which, in hindsight, was the correct decision at that time, although we likely could have obtained a higher price. Following that vote, I also opposed reducing the initiation fee for a membership drive, as I believed it would establish a precedent of offering frequent "Blue Light Specials" to the community, akin to K-Mart's practices back then. However, both decisions, made at that particular time, ultimately saved the club. In reality, we lived in a perpetual state of financial instability, always teetering on the brink of bankruptcy until those choices were made.

I would like to express my gratitude towards the numerous individuals who contributed to the club's survival after the property purchase. Doug McCann, a dedicated board member who served as secretary and president; Steve Kight, a valuable board member whose advice was always cherished; Greg Nichols, the president who guided us through the renovation of the club; Marvin Green, a dedicated board member instrumental in helping with the golf course renovation; Paul Holland, a committed board member who served as treasurer; Matt Ihnen, a dedicated board member whose attention to detail was second to none; and Mark Denton, a board member and president of later years. These individuals represent just a few examples of the many board members elected by the membership who served the club admirably over the years.

Since 1999, Rolling Hills has had the same golf professional, Kevin Rhinehart. His unwavering dedication to the club and tireless efforts in enhancing the quality of golf through lessons, tournaments, cup teams, and all aspects of the game have earned him the respect of all.

I chose to write this book as a novel, specifically a novella, since it's only 28,000 words, allowing for the inclusion of fictional elements. However, the events in which I was personally involved are portrayed as I remember them. Those who know me well will attest to my exceptional memory of details and facts.

In addition to the aforementioned details, it is important to note that the club faced various challenges over the years, including membership fluctuations, course maintenance issues, and financial struggles. Despite these obstacles, the club managed to persevere and thrive thanks to the dedication and hard work of its members.

Throughout the book, you will also find anecdotes and stories highlighting the camaraderie and sense of community that existed within the club. From memorable golf tournaments to social events and gatherings, Rolling Hills was not just a golf course but a place where friendships were forged and memories were created.

As I unravel the secrets of the club's history and share personal experiences, I hope to provide readers with a deeper understanding of the journey we embarked upon and the lessons we learned along the way. This book is a token of appreciation for the resilience and determination of the club and its members, showcasing the power of unity and the ability to overcome challenges.

So join me as we delve into the captivating world of Rolling Hills Golf and Country Club, where passion, perseverance, and love for the game amalgamate to create a truly remarkable story.

Table of Contents

About The Author iv

Preface v

Chapter 01 The Struggle For Voting Rights...............................1

Chapter 02 Long Awaited Elections 10

Chapter 03 A New Country Club...12

Chapter 04 The Opening...16

Chapter 05 The Closing..20

Chapter 06 The Uncertainty..24

Chapter 07 Southwood..27

Chapter 08 The Lake...31

Chapter 09 Another New Club..32

Chapter 10 The Men's Golf Association.................................35

Chapter 11 A New Challen ge...38

Chapter 12 More Elections 44

Chapter 13 A New Beginning...47

Chapter 14 The Fast Track..51

Chapter 15 Controversial Elections 54

Chapter 16 Post-Board Member Years 57

Chapter 17 New Greens..60

Chapter 18 A New Golf Course 65

Chapter 19 Social Activities 69

Chapter 20 Controversial Board Decision 72

Chapter 21 The Disaster..74

Chapter 22 Another Financial Crisis...78

Chapter 23 The Tobacco Controversy..82

Chapter 24 The Long-Awaited Remedy 87

Chapter 25 The Search And New Beginning..............................94

Chapter 26 Fin Tragique 96

Chapter 27 Life Goes On 102

Appendix..104

Chapter 01
THE STRUGGLE FOR VOTING RIGHTS

On a chilly Sunday morning in January 1985, the air crisp and invigorating, Rolling Hills Country Club found itself at a moment that would forever change its history.

The club's future hung in the balance as the board convened a membership meeting at the rented Executive Inn, a luxurious venue nestled on the riverfront of downtown Paducah, Ky. Their purpose was to unveil a painstakingly crafted and comprehensive proposed plan to purchase the sprawling property that the club had leased for the past three decades.

The plan carried with it a known element—an assessment of $300.00 to be levied on each member, aimed at raising the necessary down payment for the purchase and a dues increase to $50 up from $35. The anticipation was palpable as members arrived one by one, their footsteps echoing through the grand entrance hall, their breaths visible in the unforgivable winter air.

In the annals of Rolling Hills Country Club, an air of exclusivity had long woven through its boards, operating as a clandestine society where membership held no sway in the corridors of decision-making.

Yet, this pivotal gathering marked a seismic shift, a turning point destined to etch its legacy into the club's very essence. The hallowed privilege of determining the fate of their cherished country club was now bestowed upon the collective voice of its members.

Within the convention room, an electric atmosphere crackled with hope, apprehension, and a collective determination to steer the course of destiny. As members streamed into the meeting hall, palpable tension clung to the air. Conversations hummed with an undercurrent of urgency—nervous laughter and hushed discussions swirling around the proposed plan and the unexpected assessment fee. Small groups gathered, passionately debating the pros and cons, their voices tinged with the gravity of the decision.

Scanning the room, eyes darted from face to face, seeking familiar expressions that might unveil the collective sentiment. Some bore furrowed brows, faces etched with concern, mirroring the weight of the decision at hand.

In the troubled waters of uncertainty, determined expressions emerged—unyielding in their belief in the club's potential and the power of unity.

At the room's forefront, the board members stood, their typically animated faces now cloaked in uncharacteristic solemnity. The exchange of glances conveyed a shared sense of heavy responsibility. They grasped the magnitude of the moment—the fate of Rolling Hills Country Club. A haven where friendships flourished, golf swings perfected, and cherished memories forged, now teetering on the edge. Every word uttered, every detail unveiled, possessed the potential to redefine the course of history. The stakes were nothing short of the soul of a place where time and community had seamlessly woven themselves into the fabric of the club.

The next few hours would prove critical as the fate of Rolling Hills Country Club teetered on the edge. The outcome of the meeting would not only determine the club's ownership but also shape its future trajectory. The members, once passive observers, now held the power to shape the legacy of their cherished club. They had the reins in their hands now.

As the meeting was called to order, a hush fell over the room. The silence was disturbed only by the soft rustling of papers and the occasional clearing of throats. All eyes were fixed upon the board members, their words deciding the club's past, present, and future.

A few weeks before this crucial meeting, the members of our club were eagerly informed about an intriguing proposal to purchase the property. It was an exciting prospect that would require a one-time assessment of $300.00 from each member for the down payment, ensuring the acquisition of a mortgage to secure our ownership. However, as the news spread, it became apparent that there were lingering questions and concerns regarding the operation of the club and the election of the board.

Rumors started to circulate, suggesting that the operations and the appointment of board members would remain unchanged from the past. The existing system involved board members being elected by the board itself, serving for life unless they voluntarily left the club or were removed by the board.

While this lack of voting rights was tolerable when we were solely leasing the property, the situation had changed now that we were on the verge of becoming property owners. We desired the ability to have a say in electing the board members who would represent us and govern the club's operations.

With just one week remaining before the highly anticipated membership meeting, the board had yet to indicate whether they would grant the members voting rights. This uncertainty filled us with growing concern.

As a result, a group of dedicated members decided to take matters into their own hands and convene a meeting to discuss the situation. After careful deliberation, it was decided that a petition should be created and circulated amongst the members within a span of six days. The intention was to gather as many signatures as possible and present this petition to the board during the upcoming membership meeting, emphasizing the importance of granting the members voting rights.

By Tuesday, the dedicated group successfully drafted the petition, carefully crafting each word to convey the collective desire for change. The petition began to circulate, with members passionately rallying support and encouraging others to add their signatures. The response was overwhelming, as the sentiment resonated with a large number of members who were equally eager to have a voice in the club's governance.

News of the petition quickly reached the board, prompting them to hold nightly meetings in the week leading up to the membership gathering. As expected, the board members remained tight-lipped about their intentions, but leaks were bound to happen, much like in the halls of Congress. It soon became apparent that some board members were sympathetic to the cause of granting voting rights, viewing it as a progressive step forward.

However, there were others who sought to quell the rebellion forcefully, fearing a loss of control over the club's operations. These diverging opinions led to intense and heated debates during the board meetings, further fueling the anticipation for the upcoming membership gathering.

Regardless of the board's proposal, the dedicated group of members had already made up their minds. They were determined to present the petition verbally during the membership meeting, making a powerful statement and urging the board to take action. Another leak from the board hinted at their potential response – a mass walkout if the petition was read aloud. The tension reached its peak as the week drew to a close, but the dedicated members managed to collect over 180 signatures from the 500 members. Given more time, they were confident they could have obtained a substantial majority.

The meeting room at the Executive Inn was abuzz with anticipation as attendees filled the majority of the seats, leaving only a few vacant. The board, consisting of fifteen members, sat together at the front, elevated on a platform that seemed to tower over their subordinates. As the President called the meeting to order, there was a hushed silence, and all eyes turned toward the board.

After a brief introduction, the President gracefully passed the floor to another board member, who confidently stepped forward to present their proposal. The presentation was carefully crafted and skillfully delivered, captivating the audience for approximately 15 minutes. As the proposal unfolded, it became clear that the board had reached a surprising conclusion - the membership deserved voting rights, albeit partial voting rights.

Among the fifteen board members, three held officer positions - the president, the secretary, and the treasurer. The proposal outlined a plan that allowed for the election of twelve board members by the membership, while the three officers would be added to the board through a vote of the existing board members. It was evident that this approach was taken out of concern that the officers might not be elected by the membership, ensuring their protection in this way.

The attentive membership committee, recognizing the significance of this moment, elected a distinguished and successful business member to serve as their spokesperson. Following the board's presentation, they seized the opportunity to present their petition, and to the surprise of everyone, the board did not walk out - not even the most radical members, indicating a willingness to engage in a constructive dialogue.

A brief question and answer session ensued, allowing members to voice their concerns and seek clarifications. The meeting concluded with an overwhelming majority of members expressing satisfaction with the proposal. It felt like a victory for the membership, as voting rights appeared to be just around the corner - or so they believed.

In the weeks that followed, a sufficient number of members fulfilled their three hundred dollar assessment, paving the way for the finalization of the Club's purchase in July. Additionally, the board made the decision to schedule four "Quarterly Open Board Meetings" per year - January, April, July, and October. The inaugural open board meeting was eagerly anticipated in April, but to the disappointment of many, only a handful of members attended.

The chairman of the by-laws committee provided an update during the meeting, stating that the committee was diligently working on the necessary amendments to grant voting rights to the membership, with an anticipated release in the near future. However, the subsequent two quarterly open board meetings yielded similar discussions and delays.

As the January meeting arrived, exactly one year and one day had passed since the membership meeting when the decision to acquire the club was made. Yet, voting rights remained elusive, leaving members with a sense of anticipation mixed with frustration.

Over the past year, fellow members have repeatedly inquired about our plans to ensure that the board honors their promise to allow membership voting for the 12 board members. Initially, I urged patience despite not attending the first three quarterly open board meetings. However, the time had come for someone to speak up.

During the fourth quarterly open board meeting, no new information was disclosed, leaving members in the dark about the progress. Seizing the opportunity during the new business segment, I requested the floor, feeling a sense of urgency to address the issue. My question was straightforward: "Could the by-laws committee provide an update on membership voting rights?"

Depending on their response, I might have additional comments to share, hoping to shed light on the importance of fulfilling this promise. Unfortunately, the answer provided was unsatisfactory, leaving members feeling frustrated and disillusioned. The committee chairman was given the floor, and he simply stated, "David, there isn't much I can tell you except that we are working on it." I reminded him that it had been precisely one year and one day since the membership meeting, emphasizing the need for progress. Only minimal changes to the by-laws were necessary to initiate the voting process for the 12 board members, making the delay even more perplexing.

In response to the growing discontent among members, the president countered, "We all have jobs... Should Jack quit his job to rewrite the by-laws?"

This dismissive response did little to appease the concerns, as members became more engaged and started asking more questions. One member inquired about the compensation the board received for their role, hoping for transparency and accountability. To everyone's surprise, the president responded with a simple "We get our dues," leaving me with no choice but to challenge this statement. Taking an offensive posture, I couldn't resist asking if they also received a discount in the Pro shop. No surprise to me, the answer was "yes," and I could not resist saying, "Is that not compensation?"

As the meeting unfolded, it became increasingly apparent that the proceedings were not unfolding according to the regime's carefully laid plans. In the weeks leading up to this moment, I had unearthed a nugget of information—an insight into the perks enjoyed by some, if not all, board members, including complimentary entry to the highly attended New Year's Eve Dance.

Seizing the offensive, I posed a straightforward question, cutting through the veneer of denial: "Do board members receive complimentary entry to the dances?"

The president, initially vehement in his denial, found himself compelled to backtrack under the influence of a discreet tap on his arm and a whispered revelation from a fellow board member. The atmosphere crackled with tension as the acknowledgment unfolded— some board members did, in fact, attend dances without charge. The expressions on the faces of other board members betrayed a silent admission, echoing concerns of perceived unequal treatment and favoritism within the board's inner circle.

A defensive stance began to emerge among the board members, prompted by the growing discontent among the membership. They felt compelled to justify their contributions and divert attention from the brewing unease. During the audience Q&A, a voice inquired about the accessibility of board meetings to the membership, echoing a collective desire for transparency and inclusiveness.

In response, the president affirmed a general openness to meetings, with the exception of executive sessions delving into personnel matters, attempting to maintain an appearance of transparency.

At that moment, Jack, the chairperson of the by-laws committee, directed a comment toward me, expressing his frustration and desire for me to attend the meetings so that I would shut my damn mouth. Subsequently, several board members took turns boasting about their contributions to the club, highlighting their efforts in repairing the cart sheds, donating a tractor, and maintaining the swimming pool. In response, I acknowledged Dick's tractor donation and expressed gratitude for his contribution. I also thanked Sherman for his dedicated work around the club and Rick for his efforts in maintaining the pool. However, I made it clear to Jack that he owed me an apology for his disrespectful comment. Jack stood up and simply said, "David, I'm sorry."

Shortly after the meeting concluded, new by-laws were implemented with voting rights by the time the April board meeting arrived, finally fulfilling the promise made to the members.

It was not until October of 1986, approximately 22 months after the membership meeting, that we were able to elect the first three out of twelve board members, marking a significant milestone in the journey towards a more democratic and inclusive governance structure.

Chapter 02
LONG AWAITED ELECTIONS

1986 brought a wave of excitement and frenzy to the club as the first-ever election of board members by the membership approached.

It was a defining moment for the club's future, as on the second Monday in October, three out of the twelve board members would be elected directly by the members themselves. However, the current board, fearful of a potential loss of power, took preemptive measures to safeguard their positions.

Instead of assigning board terms through a fair and unbiased process, the existing board convinced three board members to voluntarily step down, effectively postponing the terms of the remaining nine members until the following year. While the three departing members had the option to run for re-election, none of them chose to do so.

This unexpected turn of events created an opportunity for fresh perspectives and new voices to join the board, as three new directors were elected to bridge the gap between the membership and the board.

The recently elected directors brought an intriguing mix of backgrounds and expertise to the board. Doug McCann, a young and soft-spoken local attorney, brought legal acumen and a keen eye for detail. Paul Holland, a Colonel in the United States Army Reserve and a member of upper management at General Tire Co., brought strong leadership skills and a strategic mindset. Notably, Virginia Davis became the club's first female director, bringing with her a wealth of experience as the president of the ladies' golf association.

However, it didn't take long for some male members to notice an interesting discrepancy in the election process. The Ladies' golf association had successfully elected one of their own to the board by casting only one vote. This revelation sparked a movement within the club, advocating for the establishment of a men's golf association. The formation of this association would ultimately lead to significant changes not only within the board but also in the course of the club's history.

This moment in the club's story marked a turning point, where the members' voices and their desire for a more inclusive and representative board began to shape the future of the club.

It was an example of democracy at its finest, which would later evolve and be adapted to the changing times and aspirations of its members.

Chapter 03
A NEW COUNTRY CLUB

In the year 1913, a young man named Francis Quimet, hailing from a humble working-class background, achieved a truly remarkable feat that sent shockwaves through the golfing world.

Against all odds, he emerged as the victor in the prestigious United States Open golf tournament, shattering the long-held notion that golf was an exclusive domain reserved only for the elite. Quimet's triumphant victory not only showcased his exceptional talent and determination but also opened the floodgates for a new generation of golfers, enlightening them to the fact that this beautiful sport could be embraced and enjoyed by people from all walks of life in the United States.

As the popularity of golf soared to unprecedented heights, the demand for more golf courses, both public and private, grew exponentially.

Sprouting up across the nation, particularly in major cities, were magnificent country clubs that catered to the burgeoning passion for the game. One particular evening in 1924, John Brunner, a highly respected executive at Standard Oil, found himself reclining in a plush armchair at his exclusive club in St. Louis, Missouri, savoring a refreshing cocktail after a satisfying round of golf.

John's mind wandered back to his humble origins in Paducah, a quaint town nestled in the western part of Kentucky, where he had spent his formative years. It was during this moment of reflection that a brilliant idea began to take shape in his mind – the vision of creating a world-class country club in his beloved hometown.

In 1925, fueled by iron-clad determination, John established Lakeview Country Club, Inc. as the entity that would oversee the construction and operations of this visionary golf and country club. Teaming up with a group of passionate investors, they meticulously crafted a comprehensive plan to bring this grand vision to life in Paducah.

Having already secured a sprawling 260 acres of pristine land just beyond the city limits in McCracken County, their next step was to enlist the services of Perry G. Maxwell, an esteemed golf course architect hailing from Ardmore, Oklahoma. Maxwell, who himself had lived in Paducah, had garnered widespread acclaim for his masterful golf course designs characterized by undulating greens and the seamless integration of natural topography to create challenging yet captivating holes.

The rugged, rolling terrain of Lakeview presented Maxwell with a blank canvas upon which he could weave his magic, designing a modern and full-length course that would test the skills of even the most seasoned players. His infectious enthusiasm for the project was imminent, as he envisioned crafting holes with unique character and intrigue, ultimately fashioning a course that would rival the very best in the country.

Maxwell boldly envisioned a future where Paducah would stand among the premier hosts for Kentucky's top golfers, earning its place on the esteemed golfing map. Notably, in 1935, Maxwell's architectural prowess culminated in the prestigious Southern Hills Country Club in Tulsa, Oklahoma, solidifying his reputation as a visionary in golf course architecture.

The genesis of a world-class golf and country club materialized as John Brunner and his dedicated team set on a transformative journey that would reshape Paducah and imprint an enduring legacy on the world of golf. In May 1926, contracts materialized for a magnificent clubhouse, a cutting-edge swimming pool, and immaculate tennis courts. Renowned craftsman A.E. (Jack) Cole secured the general contractor role, backed by Ed Hannan for plumbing and heating and Dalbey Electrical for electrical work.

The clubhouse, echoing Spanish influences, emerged as a beacon of elegance with its captivating white stucco finish and vibrant red tile roof. Perched atop a scenic hill, it commanded panoramic views of an Olympic-size swimming pool and a serene fifty-acre lake.

The main floor unfolded as an elegant haven, boasting a spacious reception room, a grand ballroom, a sophisticated dining room, a charming veranda, and a luxurious ladies' locker room. The open-style basement housed a well-equipped kitchen, a generous billiards room, a comfortable lounging area, a private director's room, and a well-appointed men's locker room.

Charming cottages were planned to dot the property, crafted for the comfort and relaxation of out-of-town guests. Lakeview proudly enlisted Chef Allen Johnson, a culinary virtuoso with 25 years of experience, to tantalize palates with exquisite cuisines.

The impeccably staffed kitchen, complemented by a dedicated parlor maid inside and outside porters, boasted modern appliances, ensuring precision in food preparation. Guests reveled in formal dining experiences in the main dining room and found a more relaxed atmosphere in the downstairs grill for casual gatherings.

The clubhouse exuded an air of refined elegance, with carefully chosen draperies, sumptuous fabrics, and opulent silk brocatelleupholstered chairs adorned with vibrant stripes. Hardwood floors, intricately patterned and graced with top-quality Wilton rugs, added a flair of warmth and sophistication. A custom-crafted oak table in the reception room stood as a focal point, commanding attention and encouraging conversation.

The lavishness extended to every detail, from the muted reds and crimson fabrics that covered the chairs to the overall design, creating an atmosphere of indulgence. Stepping into the clubhouse was a journey into refined opulence, where every element harmonized to create a space that transcended mere functionality to become a work of art.

In this world-class setting, every moment spent in the clubhouse becomes a truly memorable experience, where luxury and comfort melt seamlessly, leaving a lasting impression on all who enter.

Chapter 04
THE OPENING

Lakeview Country Club had its grand opening on September 1, 1926, at 6:30 PM. The event, eagerly anticipated by the 300 esteemed members, was a remarkable celebration of opulence and elegance.

The evening commenced with a lavish buffet dinner, tantalizing the taste buds with an array of delectable dishes prepared by renowned chefs. As the sun set and the moon ascended, casting a mystical glow over the beautifully decorated venue, the enchanting dance floor beckoned the guests to dance the night away.

The melodious tunes of Paul Rader's Orchestra, one of St. Louis' most beloved dance orchestras, filled the air, creating an atmosphere of pure merriment. The vibrant sounds of jazz and swing resonated with the hearts of the attendees, inspiring them to move to the rhythm with grace and exuberance.

Adding to the entertainment, three captivating Vaudeville acts by Keith Vaudeville Circuit, also hailing from St. Louis, graced the occasion, captivating the audience with their remarkable talent and artistry.

A heartfelt acknowledgment is due to the devoted officers of the Lakeview Corporation, led by the stalwart CEO, John Brunner. The visionary J.D. Bombback, a steady hand as president, steered the club with adept leadership. Emile D Choate, a revered figure in the community, lent her expertise as vice president, while the meticulous J. Peter Bombback, in the role of secretary, ensured the seamless operation of every facet of the club.

In tandem with these esteemed officers, Jack Brinkley and Herbert Melton stood as esteemed directors, offering invaluable guidance and support. Their collective wisdom and experience propelled Lakeview

Country Club to new heights, establishing it as the preeminent destination for socializing, recreation, and leisure in Western Kentucky.

The golf course, a masterpiece crafted by the renowned Mr. Maxwell, a luminary in course architecture, elicited a rapturous reception during its grand opening. Present at the ribbon-cutting ceremony, Mr. Maxwell, a man of unparalleled skill and vision, symbolized the dawn of a new era for Lakeview.

As the applause subsided, he took the inaugural tee shot on the first hole, marking the official opening of the course to eager members.

On the inaugural day, tee times were swiftly claimed, with both men and women in foursomes eagerly anticipating their turn to traverse the neatly manicured fairways, facing challenging hazards, and sink putts on the immaculate greens. A detailed description of each hole, including its unique characteristics and challenges, can be found in an appendix at the end of the novel, serving as a valuable guide for golfers of all skill levels.

In the early days of January 1927, Dr. P.J. Stewart assumed the esteemed position of Lakeview Country Club's inaugural President, a role unanimously bestowed upon him during the club's inaugural membership meeting. Among his responsibilities, Dr. Stewart had the honor of appointing two governors to join him on the board, acting as representatives of the membership to ensure their voices were heard and interests well-represented within the club corporation.

As winter gave way to spring in 1927, the Lakeview membership burgeoned, with nearly 400 members eagerly anticipating the upcoming golf season. The grand opening of the Olympic-sized swimming pool was set for the last week of May, promising refreshing moments of leisure and relaxation beneath the warm Kentucky sun. Soon thereafter, the unveiling of the tennis courts would provide members the chance to engage in friendly matches and hone their skills on the vibrant clay courts.

The allure of the golf and country club lifestyle captivated individuals from Paducah, Lone Oak, Heath, and Reidland, thriving despite the shadows cast by the Great War, which had concluded a mere nine years earlier. While the United States basked in the joys of life, blissfully unaware of the looming catastrophe in October 1929—the Great Depression—Lakeview Country Club became a ray of optimism and prosperity. In its serene enclave, tranquility and elegance offered comfort in a world poised for change.

Lakeview quickly became a hub of activity, hosting a variety of events that catered to the diverse interests of its members. Weddings adorned with exquisite floral arrangements and fine cuisine were celebrated in the grand ballroom, creating memories that would last a lifetime. Luncheons provided an opportunity for socializing and networking as members gathered to enjoy delectable meals while engaging in lively conversations. Small conventions and business meetings found a perfect venue at Lakeview, where the serene surroundings and impeccable service set the stage for successful collaborations and fruitful discussions.

In addition to the social events, Lakeview Country Club was renowned for its golf tournaments, attracting players from near and far. The challenging yet fair course provided a thrilling backdrop for competitive play, showcasing the skills and sportsmanship of the participants. As the club's reputation grew, so did the anticipation for the completion of the impressive 50-acre lake, a marvel of engineering and natural beauty that would further enhance the club's charm.

Looking ahead to the future, Lakeview planned to expand its offerings to cater to the needs of its discerning members. The eagerly anticipated second nine holes were scheduled to open in the spring of 1928, promising an even more remarkable golfing experience. With membership nearing capacity, set at 500 according to the by-laws, Lakeview was thriving, with individuals from all walks of life seeking to be a part of its exclusive country club.

The next phase of construction, slated for late 1929 or early 1930, would involve the creation of charming cottages for out-of-town guests to lease and enjoy the abundant amenities offered by Lakeview. These cottages, nestled amidst the picturesque landscape, would provide a home away from home, allowing guests to immerse themselves in the serenity and elegance of the country club lifestyle.

In the roaring 1920s, Lakeview Country Club transcended all boundaries, emerging as the quintessence of camaraderie, luxury, and leisure. The era's vivacity and surging economy gave rise to an atmosphere pregnant with boundless optimism, a realm where dreams took flight and possibilities stretched infinitely.

Chapter 05
THE CLOSING

The decade of the 1920s, often known as the Jazz Age or the Roaring Twenties, was a remarkable period in American history. It was characterized by unprecedented economic prosperity and significant social transformation. During this vibrant era, urban living surpassed rural living for the first time, reflecting the rapid growth of cities and the changing demographics of the nation.

The 1920s witnessed a tremendous surge in the nation's overall wealth, with the nation's wealth more than doubled between 1920 and 1929. In fact, from 1922 to 1929 alone, the GNP experienced an astonishing 40 percent growth. The economy was booming, and Americans were embracing a thriving consumer culture. People across the country shared the same music, dances, goods, and advertisements, creating a sense of unity and excitement.

However, the 1920s also brought conflicts and challenges. Prohibition, enacted in 1920, banned the production, sale, and distribution of alcoholic beverages, leading to social tensions and illegal activities. Despite the conflicts, the era was buzzing with energy and a sense of liberation.

Sadly, the decade ended with a catastrophic crash in 1929, which triggered the Great Depression, a prolonged period of economic hardship for the nation. The economic downturn had far-reaching consequences, affecting various sectors of society, including institutions like the Lakeview Country Club.

By the end of 1930, the Lakeview Country Club, once a thriving establishment since its inception in 1926, experienced a significant decline in membership due to financial difficulties. Many individuals

THE CLUB

could no longer afford the fees, leading to layoffs and a struggle to maintain the services the club had once provided.

In an attempt to salvage the situation, the Lakeview Corporation decided to sell its assets to John D. Bombback, who not only served as the president of the corporation but also the president of the City National Bank. The transaction involved a payment of $1400 and the assumption of all debts. Despite Mr. Bombback's efforts, including transforming the club into a semi-private establishment and offering daily facility use, the club's financial condition continued to deteriorate.

An advertisement in the Paducah Sun-Democrat highlighted these desperate measures taken to generate much-needed revenue. While these initiatives brought in some income, they proved insufficient to prevent the eventual insolvency of the Lakeview Country Club. As a result, the club filed for bankruptcy in the fall of 1932, marking the end of an era and reflecting the profound impact of the economic downturn on various aspects of American Life.

On the fateful Wednesday of October 28, 1932, the esteemed City National Bank, a community cornerstone, fell into the grip of a receiver. Mr. Bombback, a dedicated luminary with an extraordinary 40-year tenure at the bank, commenced his journey as a humble messenger boy at 16. Through remarkable perseverance, he ascended the ranks, achieving the pinnacle as the esteemed President in 1917. Beyond his influence in banking, he also served as McCracken Co.'s treasurer for an impressive two decades.

As the morning sun dawned on the anticipatory Friday of October 30th, Mr. Bombback started his day with a determined purpose. Informing his son of his intention to travel to Lakeview Country Club for a leisurely stroll around the enchanting grounds, a sanctuary where he would often find release from his thoughts. However, as the sun began its descent, worry marked its presence in his family's hearts. His absence, unusual for the responsible and punctual Mr. Bombback, prompted immediate reporting to local authorities in search of answers.

The next day, hope flickered as Mr. Bombback's car was discovered at Lakeview Country Club. Silent and abandoned, it stood in stark contrast to the vibrant life that once animated its seats. Unfortunately, the prior night's severe thunderstorm had erased potential clues, leaving no traces of Mr. Bombback's whereabouts. No footprints, no signs of struggle. The storm had wiped away evidence, leaving investigators both perplexed and deeply concerned.

While depression stemming from the bank's insolvency hinted at the possibility of suicide, the absence of concrete evidence within the car cast doubt on this theory. No letters or notes, no farewell messages emerged. Moreover, no signs of foul play or struggle existed. The mysterious disappearance of Mr. Bombback lingered as an enigma, a haunting puzzle for the community.

Days melded into weeks, weeks into months, and months into years, yet the truth behind Mr. Bombback's disappearance remained elusive. The passage of time deepened the mystery, adding layers of intrigue and wonder. Two decades slipped away, and still, no answers emerged.

The memory of Mr. Bombback and the unanswered questions surrounding his vanishing act wove into local folklore, creating a trail of curiosity that stayed through the years in the community's collective memory.

Chapter 06
THE UNCERTAINTY

In mid-1933, McCracken County took legal action against John Bombback's estate, seeking $10,000 in damages for his alleged misuse of county funds during his tenure as treasurer. The lawsuit claimed that the funds were wrongfully utilized to settle the bills of Lakeview, a once-thriving establishment that served various purposes during the following decade. It transformed from a nightclub to a campsite for idle youths and even housed German prisoners during World War II.

Nestled within the captivating landscapes of the Lakeview Country Club, Lakeview was an opportunity recognized by the astute minds of the U.S. Government. They saw beyond the rolling greens and majestic clubhouse, envisioning a haven where idle youths could learn, grow, and thrive.

In the spring of 1934, the government's plan came to fruition as Lakeview opened its doors as a camp for transient boys. Here, amidst the verdant fairways and shimmering pool waters, they received not just practical instruction in agriculture, gardening, and craftsmanship but also a sense of purpose and direction for their futures. With aspirations as vast as the sprawling landscape before them, the camp welcomed boys from every corner of the country, uniting them in a shared journey of discovery and growth.

As the country's economy was finally recovering from the depths of The Great Depression and 11 months before December 7th, 1941, a date that lives in infamy that propelled us into WWII, an idea emerged in the minds of some prominent businessmen in Paducah. Led by I.H. Strickland, this group acquired the Lakeview Property with a noble intention: to restore it as a premier golf country club.

After undergoing meticulous renovations, the club was reborn as Forest Hills Country Club, capturing the essence of elegance and luxury reminiscent of the opulent 1920s. The grand opening, held on the evening of April 18, 1941, became a memorable affair with a splendid dance featuring the musical styling of Ray Johnson and his orchestra from St. Louis, Missouri. The club witnessed an overwhelming attendance of over 300, marking its resurgence with resounding success. Forest Hills once again became a favored destination for golf enthusiasts, swimmers, and social events.

But it was in the throes of uncertainty, against the backdrop of World War II, that Forest Hills faced its greatest challenge. Gasoline rationing gripped the nation, making it difficult for members to reach the cherished club. Still, in the trials of wartime, Forest Hills stood steadfast but had to temporarily close its doors for the duration of the war. Its legacy remained preserved in the hearts of those who cherished its memory.

In the wake of the war's continued uncertainty, new chapters unfolded in Lakeview's storied history. December 11, 1944, marked a pivotal moment as Chester McGuire, a man of vision and ambition, took hold of the sprawling 300-acre property. While his plans for its future remained uncertain, the echoes of his footsteps through the clubhouse corridors spoke of endless possibilities and untold adventures yet to unfold. Further adding to the historical context, McGurie leased the clubhouse and surrounding grounds to house German prisoners during the war, leaving a lasting imprint on the site's legacy.

Then, in the balmy days of June 1950, Wells Heath emerged as a hopeful figure, purchasing the property at auction with a promising resolve. With dreams as vast as the open skies above, he wanted to breathe new life into the former Lakeview estate, transforming it into a vibrant community of residential homes.

Today, through the pages of history, the story of Lakeview remains a symbol of the enduring spirit and the indomitable will of those who dared to dream. Unfolded by time, it has been a tale of transformation, triumph, and timeless charm.

Chapter 07
SOUTHWOOD

In July 1952, Robert R. Guthrie from Guthrie Investment Company in New York and St. Petersburg purchased the Lakeview property. Mr. Guthrie stated that he bought it as an investment, with plans to graze some cattle on the tract. He also envisioned developing a new subdivision consisting of five to ten-acre tracts exclusively for homes in the $40,000 range. The proposed subdivision would feature the current clubhouse and swimming pool for social events, adding another chapter in the history of owners of the Lakeview property.

Shortly after, a group of investors approached Mr. Guthrie with an offer to lease the property and establish a new country club. Intrigued by the idea, Mr. Guthrie spent a few months working on the land and exploring the potential of a country club on the property. Impressed by the investors' vision and determination, he agreed to lease the property to them.

Without delay, a group of investors joined forces to establish Southwood Country Club Inc., swiftly completing all necessary paperwork. Eager to grow their membership, they called upon interested individuals to attend a meeting on Sunday, December 21st. At this gathering, they offered stock shares priced at $250, covering first-year dues and applicable to the entire family, with a one-share limit per family. The response exceeded expectations, with the club reaching its goal of 200 charter members by early March 1953. Finally, on Wednesday, April 8, 1953, a 25-year lease agreement was inked between Guthrie Investment Company and Southwood Country Club. With this monumental contract secured, the club shifted its focus to refurbishing the clubhouse and preparing the initial nine holes of the golf course.

In April, Southwood made an exciting announcement that had golf enthusiasts buzzing with anticipation. They revealed their plans to introduce a new type of grass to their fairways - the Tiffine Bermuda. This remarkable grass variety is the result of a crossbreeding experiment between Tiflawn and South African Bermuda, combining the best traits of both.

Extensive tests conducted by the esteemed Georgia Coastal Plain Experiment Station have shown that Tiffine Bermuda boasts a finer grass blade compared to common Bermuda, giving the course a more pristine and luxurious appearance. Not only that, but Tiffine Bermuda has also proven to exhibit equal drought resistance, ensuring the course remains vibrant and lush even during dry spells.

What sets Tiffine Bermuda apart is its remarkable resilience to cold weather conditions. While common Bermuda may struggle to bounce back after harsh winters, Tiffine Bermuda stands strong, showcasing its superior adaptability and endurance. This makes it an excellent choice for Southwood, as they strive to provide golfers with superior fairway conditions for an optimal golfing experience.

However, despite the promising announcement, it remains unclear whether the introduction of Tiffine Bermuda was ever implemented. The latter club in this location, Rolling Hills Country Club, has always proudly claimed their fairways showcased common Bermuda fairways.

As the highly anticipated grand opening of Southwood Country Club loomed on the horizon, anticipation crackled in the air like static electricity before a storm. The members, along with a dedicated cadre of contracted workers, poured their souls into every nook and cranny of the clubhouse, swimming pool, and, most importantly, the carefully manicured golf course. Each blade of grass seemed to bow in reverence to the impending event, while every corner of the clubhouse gleamed with the promise of opulence and grandeur.

With an eye for detail sharper than the keenest blade, Southwood aimed not just to impress but to leave an indelible mark on the hearts and minds of its guests. The stage was set for an unforgettable experience, one of luxury and leisure that would forever be remembered.

True to its vision, Southwood quickly blossomed into a bustling hub of activity, its grounds alive with the laughter and chatter of like-minded souls. Weddings, luncheons, small conventions, dances, and, of course, golf tournaments became the hallmark of Southwood's social calendar, each event infused with the spirit of celebration and camaraderie that defined the club.

Through the economic boom sweeping across the United States, the future of Southwood seemed as bright as the midday sun, its promise of prosperity and enduring legacy drawing members from far and wide. But, as fate would have it, a shadow lurked on the horizon, casting doubt upon the club's newfound success.

With the abruptness of a lightning strike on a clear summer day, disaster struck on September 23, 1955. Without warning, the Guthrie Investment Company launched a legal onslaught against Southwood, accusing the club of late rent payments and demanding recompense for supposed transgressions against the terms of their lease agreement.

Sheriff's deputies descended upon the club like harbingers of doom, serving an order of attachment and locking up the clubhouse immediately. The accusations flew like arrows on a battlefield, each one piercing the heart of Southwood's dreams with unforgiving precision.

But shockingly, Southwood stood firm, defiant in the face of injustice. With a resolute spirit, the club launched a counteroffensive, filing a $100,000 countersuit against the Guthrie Investment Company, denying the allegations of wrongdoing and seeking reparation for the harm inflicted upon them.

The wheels of justice turned slowly, grinding forward with all the ponderous weight of fate itself. Circuit Judge Holland G. Bryan implored both parties to seek a resolution, urging them to set aside their grievances in the name of the greater good.

But despite the judge's entreaties, the legal battle raged on, each side digging in their heels like soldiers entrenched on the battlefield. The pre-trial conference yielded no resolution, and the hearing continued on November 2nd, showing the lengths to which both parties were willing to go to defend their honor and integrity.

Finally, in May 1956, an out-of-court settlement was reached. It was a bittersweet victory for Southwood. Though they received a substantial cash settlement, the damage had been done. The Guthrie Company had already moved on and had entered into a contract with another group. A new country club had been in operation since April, leaving Southwood to pick up the shattered remnants of their dreams and build a new path forward.

As the dust settled on this issue, Southwood stood firm despite its shaken identity. Despite the trials and tribulations that had befallen them, the club's brief existence was one of perseverance, a nod to those who dared to dream big and reach for the stars.

Chapter 08
THE LAKE

The 50-acre lake, known for its picturesque beauty, had been gradually drying up since its construction in late 1928. As plans were being made for the design of the second nine holes at Southwood, a bold decision was made to drain the lake completely and incorporate this area into the golf course. This deviated from Perry Maxwell's original layout but promised to bring a unique challenge to golf enthusiasts.

However, as the lake was being drained, an unexpected discovery sent shockwaves through the community. Human skeletal remains were unearthed, casting a somber shadow over the project. The McCracken County Sheriff's Department was promptly notified, launching a detailed investigation, recovery, and analysis to determine the cause of death and identify the remains. Recognizing the need for expertise and specialized personnel, the state police were summoned to handle the delicate recovery process, ensuring every step was taken to minimize the risk of errors.

After what seemed like an eternity, the breakthrough came. Dental records were used to confirm the identity of the remains, revealing that they belonged to none other than Mr. John D. Bombback, the missing former President of Lakeview Country Club and President of City National Bank.

It was a sudden, shocking revelation, as Mr. Bombback had mysteriously disappeared in October 1932, shortly after the bank went into receivership. The two-decade-long unsolved mystery surrounding his vanishing act had finally found its conclusion, bringing closure to those who had wondered about his fate for so long.

Chapter 09
ANOTHER NEW CLUB

Rolling Hills, Inc. was established as a non-profit corporation with the primary objective of managing the brand-new Rolling Hills Country Club. This prestigious club, located on the grounds of the former Lakeview Country Club, which was carefully designed to offer an unparalleled experience, aims to provide a haven for individuals seeking a harmonious blend of leisure and community. The founder and President of Rolling Hills is Paul Friedlander, a former city commissioner and friend of Guthrie.

For smooth operations and effective decision-making, a permanent operating board comprising ten members, including Friedlander, was established. This diverse and experienced team is dedicated to creating an environment that caters to the various needs of the club's esteemed members. Notably, this new organization operated independently from the old Southwood Corporation, signaling a fresh start in the region's social and recreational era.

In anticipation of welcoming potential members, an exciting open house event is scheduled for Sunday, providing an exclusive opportunity to tour Rolling Hills Country Club's state-of-the-art facilities. Prospective members will witness firsthand the delicately designed spaces and amenities that exude luxury and sophistication.

To facilitate membership, a reasonable fee structure has been introduced. The membership fee, currently set at $25 plus tax, grants individuals access to a world-class club experience. Additionally, monthly dues of $12 guarantee ongoing access to exceptional services and facilities. However, it has been announced that starting in June, the membership fee will increase to $50, reflecting the club's commitment to dedicated enhancement and growth.

Amid the transition, there are stories circulating about the establishment of Rolling Hills. Rumors suggest that Friedlander's decision to implement a permanent board without granting voting rights or say in club operations to the membership may have been influenced by a conversation with Guthrie. The sudden closure of Southwood by Guthrie, followed by the prompt initiation of Rolling Hills before the lawsuit settlement, has sparked curiosity.

Also, three months after Rolling Hills' inception, Guthrie reached a substantial cash settlement with Southwood, leading to speculation about a potential backroom deal between Guthrie and Friedlander. Nonetheless, Southwood is now in the past, and Rolling Hills is setting on a promising future.

During the first 15 years of operation, Friedlander, with the expertise and labor of the membership, made significant enhancements to the club. With the collective efforts of passionate members, an additional nine holes were carefully constructed, enhancing the already impressive course.

In 1963, my family relocated to Paducah, eagerly joining Rolling Hills, where the monthly dues remained at a modest $12. Although the club's by-laws initially authorized a membership level of 500, it remains unclear when this threshold was reached. However, by 1975, when I became a member through my parents' membership, the club boasted an impressive roster of 500 members, with a growing waiting list for prospective members. Surprisingly, the monthly dues at that time amounted to a mere $15, offering exceptional value for the club's outstanding offerings.

While Rolling Hills may not have been regarded as a top-rated golf course, it undeniably offered an unparalleled value proposition for the $15 monthly dues. The fact that the board was self-perpetuating did not raise concerns among the membership, primarily because the property was not collectively owned.

However, in 1968, Mr. Guthrie's passing marked a significant turning point as the estate began increasing the monthly lease amount. By 1978, the dues had escalated to $25 per month, and by 1985, the year we purchased the property, the dues were $35, reflecting the club's continuous commitment to providing an exceptional experience for its esteemed members.

Chapter 10
THE MEN'S GOLF ASSOCIATION

In December of 1986, a set of by-laws was adopted, and officers were elected to form the inaugural Men's Golf Association. The first meeting was brimming with excitement and enthusiasm as more than 50 men came together. Leading the association was Bob Swisher, a prominent sportscaster from the local NBC affiliate television station, who served as the first president. Charlie Loyd, Vice President, and Vince Renaud, Secretary/Treasurer, accompanied him.

Committees were established, and the social committee, led by Tom Rasche and John Floyd Jr., wasted no time in organizing a Super Bowl Party for the end of January. In previous years, the Super Bowl lacked excitement for club members, as there was no organized gathering. Two years ago, only four people showed up to watch the game, and last year, a meager attendance of 10 was achieved through our own efforts. Determined to make our first event a success, the newly formed Men's Golf Association committee decided to create a buzz by introducing a "Two Thousand Dollar Big Board" with eight payouts, accompanied by a delicious shrimp dinner. The dinner featured jumbo boiled shrimp, Jambalaya, and John Deboe's famous red beans and rice, all for a mere $8.00. The party surpassed all expectations, with over 100 members in attendance. And so the Men's Golf Association began its journey with a resounding success.

I was appointed to lead the tournament committee, which was responsible for organizing our monthly tournaments. Previously, the club's board had overseen these events, but they willingly passed on the responsibility. We wanted to infuse new excitement by introducing different formats such as scrambles, better ball, best ball, and modified alternating shots. To efficiently manage the committee, I assigned each member to oversee one or more tournaments. While the entire committee would meet to discuss, offer suggestions, and assist with specific tournaments, each member took charge of ensuring the success of their assigned event. As a result, tournament participation increased by 30%.

The board voluntarily relinquished its role in managing the handicap committee, and I was appointed as its chair. Despite golf's reputation for integrity and honesty, some members were found to be falsifying their scores to manipulate their handicaps, giving them an unfair advantage in tournaments. To address this issue and enhance transparency, I implemented procedures to ensure compliance with the mandatory "Equitable Stroke Adjustment" for an official USGA handicap score, aiming to restore integrity to our club's handicap system.

Unlike other clubs in our area, which simply submitted scores to GHIN for a handicap card, we meticulously followed all USGA rules, making us the sole club with a legitimate handicap system for three years. Upholding the integrity of our handicap system was a fundamental requirement imposed by the USGA, and our committee took pride in fulfilling it. While this rule might have been overlooked by many clubs, we distinguished ourselves through our commitment.

We had a dedicated handicap committee responsible for administering and maintaining the system, whereas many clubs relied on individuals lacking comprehensive knowledge of USGA rules. Our thorough approach ensured fairness and accuracy for all members, setting us apart as a club that valued the true spirit of the handicap system.

After implementing these changes, our Men's Golf Association not only boasted a thriving community of passionate golfers but also emphasized fairness, camaraderie, and sportsmanship. Our adherence to USGA rules set us apart, earning us a reputation for integrity and genuine fairness in our handicap system.

In 1992, the newly elected club President sought to dissolve the Men's Golf Association, citing concerns about its influence. However, it's important to recognize the association's significant contributions to the club. From 1987 to 1992, the association financed the construction of the club's first professionally constructed practice green, organized social activities, and initiated the Men's Member Guest Tournament, which remains the club's largest event. The association also financially supported various golf course projects, enhancing the overall member experience.

The association generated revenue through social activities, tournaments, and membership dues. Membership included access to the handicap system, promising fairness for all. Unfortunately, separating handicap responsibilities from the association led to membership decline and compromised adherence to USGA rules, jeopardizing our official USGA handicap status.

In the face of these challenges, the Men's Golf Association played a vital role in the club. Over time, as the club met members' needs, interest in the association declined, leading to its dissolution. Many board members, who had served with dedication, emerged from the association, underscoring its contributions to club governance.

The Men's Golf Association's story demonstrates the impact of dedicated individuals on a club. Though the association no longer exists, its legacy endures through friendships, memories, and positive changes in our golfing community.

Chapter 11
A NEW CHALLENGE

In February 1987, the Secretary of the club, who had played a pivotal role in its operations, resigned and relocated to Nashville, TN. This particular board position was one of the protected positions by the regime rather than being elected by the membership. The sudden departure left a void that needed to be filled urgently. To address this, the board decided to appoint Mr. Doug McCann, one of the three newly elected members to the board by the membership the previous October, as the new Secretary. Interestingly, this appointment created another vacancy as Mr. McCann's elected position on the board became available.

This unexpected turn of events triggered a series of events that would shape the course of the club's future. One of the candidates who emerged as a potential replacement was Wilbur Dunker. However, many members harbored doubts and believed that Wilbur had been chosen by the previous administration, raising concerns about his independence. Despite Wilbur's amicable nature and his successful leadership of a recent member project to rebuild the retaining wall between the swimming pool and the tennis courts, some perceived his candidacy as lacking autonomy.

As the election neared, scheduled to align with the quarterly membership/board meeting in July, the window for nominations was closing. With just a few days left, a conversation between Charlie Loyd and myself took an unexpected turn. I suggested to Charlie that he should consider running for the board, given his passion for the club's affairs. In response, Charlie astutely suggested that I, myself, would be the most formidable candidate against Wilbur. Initially, I brushed off Charlie's suggestion, as I had never envisioned myself as part of the board. However, after much contemplation and soul-searching, I had a change of heart and decided to nominate myself.

Upon examining the club's by-laws, I realized that the nomination committee was not obligated to endorse my candidacy. To address this potential hurdle, I explored an alternative pathway outlined within the by-laws. This involved gathering signatures from 10 regular voting members on a petition, which would then be submitted to the nominating committee as a formal nomination. Determined to present a comprehensive platform for my candidacy, I included a detailed outline of my ideas and the direction I believed the club should take. This approach marked a significant departure from tradition, as it was the first time a candidate had presented a petition with a platform to provide transparency and clarity on their intentions.

Soon, the nomination deadline approached, and anticipation grew within the club. The stage was set for an important election that would shape the club's future trajectory. Little did I know at that moment that this decision to nominate myself would set in motion a series of events that would forever change the history of the club and my own personal journey within it.

DAVID EDWARDS

PETITION

We, the undersigned Members of Rolling Hills Country Club, do hereby nominate David G. Edwards as Candidate for Executive Board Member of Rolling Hills County Club.

Having been a Member, in good standing, of Rolling Hills Country Club since 1979, and having shown interest in all activities and order of business thereof; we feel that David will be an asset to the present Board. The following is the platform of our Candidate:

1. I plan to run as a "Dues Paying" Board Member. It is my personal belief that Board Members should pay their dues just as every other Member does, especially at the present time when the Club is struggling with a large indebtedness; major improvements are needed; and the Membership is less than 500, with no waiting list.

2. I believe in an Open Policy with the General Membership and if elected will strive to put this into action.

3. I have felt a great need for improvement in the relationship of the Executive Board and the General Membership, and I will make every effort to bring this into reality.

4. I believe a plan of action should be developed and goals set by the Board for improving and upgrading the three recreational facilities of Rolling Hills Country Club, to-wit: Golf Course, Tennis Courts and Swimming Pool.

CONCLUSION: If elected, I pledge to work toward the above mentioned goals and will otherwise be open for suggestions regarding improving the quality of Rolling Hills Country Club to make it a better facility for its present Members and more attractive to prospective Members.

Respectfully submitted:

THE CLUB

The day of the election was a mix of excitement and anxiety for me. While I had the support of enough members to win, I could not shake off the feeling that the opposing side might try to manipulate the results.

I had several members making calls on my behalf, and I personally made around 80 to 100 calls that day. My only comfort was the fact that Paul Holland, a Colonel in the Reserve Corps of the United States Army, was the chairman of the election committee, and I trusted his integrity completely. When I arrived at the club that evening, it became evident that the opposing side had also been working hard to rally support. Even members who rarely visited the club, except for the Christmas Eggnog Party and the Derby Party, had suddenly emerged to back Wilbur. As the meeting progressed, I glanced around the room, mentally counting votes and questioning Paul's unwavering integrity. Just then, Paul emerged from the basement with the election committee, ready to announce the official results.

My heart raced, and fear enveloped my mind, worried that they would somehow steal the election. Paul stood up and declared, "The winner and new board member is David Edwards."

Did I hear correctly? Did he really say my name? Time seemed to slow down as I struggled to process Paul's words. And then, a thunderous applause erupted in the ballroom, and it finally dawned on me that this was not a dream but reality. We had triumphed over the opposing side, dealing them a devastating blow. I'm sure it must have felt like a thorn plunged deep into their hearts.

Three days later, I found myself attending my first board meeting as a director. This meeting was called specifically to address an issue that had arisen within the Men's Golf Association. Our president began the meeting by distributing copies of two proposals from the association outlining potential solutions for implementing an irrigation system. As he was handing out the proposals, he remarked,

"From what I understand, no one here, except David, is familiar with these proposals!"

I was about to respond, pointing out that anyone who had attended the association meeting in June would have received a copy of these proposals. However, the president interrupted me, saying, "I don't want to hear from you right now, sir!" Recognizing that I had not been given the floor, I nodded and patiently allowed others to voice their concerns until it was my turn to speak.

The golf course had endured a harsh spring and summer in 1987, with minimal rainfall, resulting in significant damage. The Men's Golf Association had brainstormed ideas on how to finance an irrigation system, and a couple of members had even presented written proposals with cost estimates and potential funding options. These proposals were shared at the June meeting, with the suggestion that we review them and reconvene at the next meeting in July to discuss our preferred course of action.

Unfortunately, none of the board members had attended the MGA meeting, leaving them unaware of the association's intentions. It became apparent that several board members harbored negative sentiments towards the MGA as they began expressing their frustrations. "This could be the downfall of our club," one member exclaimed. "It's time we assert our authority and show the MGA who's really running this club!" exclaimed another member. These were just a couple of the derogatory remarks made that evening until, finally, one member asked for my input.

Once I presented the facts about the proposals, the board members' attitudes started to shift. Instead of summoning the MGA officers to assert our control, it was decided to invite them to a meeting with the board to discuss these proposals in detail. This approach not only allowed for a more collaborative and inclusive decision-making process but also demonstrated a willingness to work together toward the betterment of the club.

On the following Thursday, a highly anticipated and pivotal meeting occurred with the esteemed Board and the dedicated MGA officers. The atmosphere buzzed with anticipation as valuable information was exchanged during the meeting, leaving everyone feeling optimistic and positive. This gathering marked a significant milestone in the club's history, as it was the first time the board warmly invited all members to actively participate in discussions and share their thoughts and perspectives.

To everyone's surprise, it was revealed that the club was facing unforeseen financial difficulties despite its illustrious past and initial promise. It was astonishing to learn that even with an impressive membership of 500 individuals and an additional 200 prospective members eagerly waiting, financial challenges persisted. These issues arose after the club's acquisition in 1985 when it appeared poised for continued success and growth.

The board, with its wisdom and experience, had not anticipated such a drastic decline to less than 400 members after implementing a $300.00 assessment to acquire the club. Over the past two years, the board experimented with various strategies to attract new members, but their efforts yielded limited success. One notable approach was introducing a corporate membership class, allowing corporations to purchase a corporate membership and giving their employees an opportunity to join the club without having to pay an initiation fee. While this initially led to 25 new members, many resigned once the golf season ended, lacking personal investment in the club.

It's now clear that without a substantial revenue increase, major improvements and transformative changes will remain elusive goals. The challenges ahead require a comprehensive and strategic approach to ensure Rolling Hills' long-term sustainability and prosperity.

Chapter 12
MORE ELECTIONS

The upcoming election for three additional board members was just around the corner. As per the by-laws, the yearly election was scheduled to take place during the October quarterly board meeting. While playing golf in early August with my friend and fellow board member, Doug McCann, who held the position that I had been elected to fill, he revealed something troubling.

You may recall that Doug had been appointed to one of the three protected positions, which resulted in his elected position becoming available and subsequently filled by my election. During the August board meeting, we were tasked with determining the conclusion of three board members' terms. Doug revealed that the current board had intentions to nominate me for re-election in October. This decision was based on their prior discussion that any newly elected board member filling an unexpired term would automatically be considered a candidate in the annual election.

I brought to Doug's attention that since I had assumed his original term and he was now one of the three safeguarded board members required to stand for election every year during the March board meeting, this would breach the promise made to the membership. If the board proceeded with its plan to have me run again in October, it would mean that only 11 board members would have been elected in the span of four years instead of the required 12. Doug, who possesses intelligence and reason, swiftly acknowledged the validity of my point. With Doug as an ally and the accuracy of my assessment, I felt assured of prevailing in this argument.

The August board meeting proceeded as planned, without any new revelations or notable changes in revenue. The discussion then turned to the upcoming board member elections in October. The president initiated the conversation by announcing that David's position would naturally be one of the three up for election and inquired if any other board members were willing to put forth their positions. I requested and was granted the opportunity to speak, expressing my confusion regarding the necessity of my position being put up for re-election. I reminded the board that I had been elected in July to fill the unexpired term of Doug, who had been elected the previous October for a 4-year term. The president promptly asserted that this decision had been predetermined by the board. I presented my arguments, and Doug concurred with my assessment. It seemed that I had successfully made my case until E.F. Hutton spoke.

Steve Kight, a highly regarded and soft-spoken president of a local bank, was E.F. Hutton in our board room. His words carried weight, and he voiced his opposition to my argument. A back-and- forth ensued for a few minutes until Doug once again affirmed the correctness of my assessment. Once more, victory was on my side, and now we need to identify three board members who have not yet served terms and are not among the three protected members to run in the October election.

In October, three members of the men's golf association enthusiastically entered the race for directors: Larry Hill, Vince Renaud, and Cletus Poat. Each of these candidates presented the nominating committee with a petition letter outlining their platforms. Interestingly, one of the candidates was so impressed with my petition that he requested a copy and sought permission to incorporate some of the ideas into his own petition. I gladly shared the document, only to discover that he changed just one thing – the name!

Surprisingly, no one in the club seemed to notice the striking similarity with my previous petition three months earlier, leading me to believe that I was the sole observer of this act of plagiarism.

Despite this, all three candidates secured positions on the board, and the MGA emerged victorious once again. The practice of presenting a petition and platform for candidacy gained popularity, enabling members to evaluate and make informed decisions, and persisted for several years. However, over time, its appeal waned, and today, candidates are mainly nominated by the nominating committee. Their names are posted in the clubhouse and the monthly bulletin, as required by the by-laws. Unfortunately, this leaves the membership with little information to assess when deciding whom to vote for.

Chapter 13
A NEW BEGINNING

The board underwent a significant transformation in recent times due to the past two general elections and a special election. The incumbent board members were given a clear message: shape up or ship out.

On the eve of the inaugural board meeting for the new directors, I engaged in a conversation with the three newly elected directors about the potential committee appointments that would be made by the President. The board at RHCC diverged from the norm of other country clubs. Our responsibilities went beyond monthly policy-setting and long-term planning; we were actively involved in committee work throughout the month.

Unlike other clubs, Rolling Hills lacked a Club Manager or a Golf Pro, as financial constraints prevented us from filling these positions. The swimming pool committee, in particular, was a role that most board members avoided due to the extensive tasks of opening, maintaining, and winterizing the pool, as well as overseeing the lifeguards. This committee assignment served as a means for the President to discipline board members he disfavored. Recognizing Vince Renaud's retirement status and his desire to enhance his standing at Rolling Hills, I suggested to Vince that he would be an ideal fit for the swimming pool committee. Vince promptly approached the President and secured the position of committee chairman. I'm sure I dodged a bullet as the President asked me to be his co-chair, and I agreed to assist Vince in procuring any needed repairs, but I did not have the time to do any repair work or manage the lifeguards.

My primary responsibility was to lead the children's activities committee. I accepted this assignment with some apprehension, as I informed the President that I didn't have any children. To my surprise, he revealed that he, too, had chaired the committee without having any children of his own. Despite understanding his motive for assigning me this role, I assured him that I would exceed expectations.

Bob Morris, a fellow board member and a friend who happened to be dating my mother-in-law, offered some advice. "David," he said, "the most effective way to manage this committee's activities is to find a mother who is genuinely interested because she has young children and let her take charge."

However, I decided not to follow his suggestion. Instead, drawing from my previous experience as the chairman of the MGA tournaments, I assembled a committee comprising both men and women who shared a passion for improving the experience of the children at Rolling Hills. Together, we aimed to make Rolling Hills a better place for the children of our club.

The committee convened to deliberate on past and future endeavors. Among the existing activities, the Easter Egg Hunt took precedence as the inaugural event of the year. Upon my wife's suggestion, we introduced a coloring contest, which quickly became a cherished tradition among the children. Later, we inaugurated a new activity called Kids Day at the onset of summer, alongside the customary swimming contest to conclude the summer season. Other activities included the Halloween party and Christmas party for the children, as well as the Valentine dance and Christmas dance for the teens. Drawing from my prior experience with the MGA tournament committee, I adopted a management approach where each member chaired an activity, with the remainder of the committee providing assistance.

Cindy Metzger led the Kids Day initiative, ensuring children enjoyed games, prizes, and refreshments. Kathy and David Jenks, Valerie and John Kortz, and Dana and Coy Womble played vital roles in its success. Kids Day remained a perennial favorite for years, cherished by Rolling Hills' children and appreciated by parents for the committee's efforts to enhance their club experience.

As the New Year began, the club faced a significant decision. A local building contractor offered to buy 150 acres of undeveloped property for $265,000, proposing to turn it into a residential subdivision. Uncertainty surrounded the property's true value, leading to the formation of a committee comprising five board members, including the President. The committee held confidential meetings and negotiations, shielding their discussions from the rest of the board to navigate the decision-making process.

Despite discussions during board meetings about the property's value, the committee did not take action to acquire sensitive information about the property's value except to obtain a per acre value of undeveloped property from a commercial realty company. Feeling unsettled, I suggested assessing the property's value from a developer's perspective. However, the committee's recommendation to accept Phil Higdon's offer of $307,000, including an additional 15 acres, was based on the commercial realtor's estimate per acre.

Despite presenting my assessment suggesting the property's value might be worth between $450,000 and $600,000, the committee dismissed it, relying on gut feeling rather than substantive reasoning. The board, except for me, voted to accept the offer. Concerned about the lack of information, I argued for further research to ensure the best outcome for the club.

At the membership meeting, the board's recommendation to sell the property was met with enthusiasm and trust from attendees, who voted overwhelmingly in favor. Only time would tell if this decision would be celebrated as a stroke of genius or regretted as a missed opportunity. Regardless, this decision paved the way for a well-respected developer, Phil Higdon, to develop a new residential subdivision. His vision was to create a subdivision that would seamlessly blend with the existing golf course, enhancing its appeal and potentially attracting new members to the club.

During discussions at the next board meeting following the completion of the sale, there was a lively debate over how to allocate the proceeds of the sale. Some board members proposed allocating a majority, if not the entirety, of the sale funds to club enhancements, emphasizing the importance of investing in our facilities to attract and retain members.

Frank Hargrove, a longstanding member and avid tennis player, passionately argued that constructing two new tennis courts would not only benefit the club but would also elevate its status in the community. I couldn't help but wonder if the bank that held our debt would have allowed such a diversion of funds. Ultimately, we did not have to find out the bank's position as the majority of board members agreed to allocate a significant portion to debt reduction.

Another significant decision made by the board at this time was to launch a membership drive offering a reduced initiation fee, which resulted in over 100 new members eagerly joining our club. This allowed us to reach the club's maximum membership level for the first time since acquiring the property in 1985. The successful membership drive, combined with the property sale, provided the club with a solid foundation for improvements and future growth.

The journey from the membership meeting to consider purchasing the club property in 1985 to reaching this point was loaded with challenges and successes. However, it also demonstrated the collective vision and commitment of the board, staff, and membership. Reflecting on these achievements, we see limitless possibilities for the club's future prosperity.

Chapter 14
THE FAST TRACK

As the winter of 1988 transitioned into spring, the future of the club appeared brighter than ever before. The relationship between the membership and the board had significantly improved thanks to an open policy and the election of 6 board members by the membership. The sale of the 165 acres for a residential subdivision decreased our indebtedness substantially, and the additional revenue generated from the increase in membership allowed us to make long-awaited improvements to our facilities.

Exciting changes were already underway. Two new tennis courts were being constructed, promising enhanced playing experiences for our members. The installation of state-of-the-art lighting to replace the outdated lighting would ensure that the courts would have increased use during evening hours. However, our golf course was in dire need of a complete irrigation system. Currently, we could only manually water the greens using city water, which was far from efficient.

Apart from the course improvements, the condition of our clubhouse was also a top priority. The original clay tile roof, which had faithfully served us for over six decades, was showing signs of wear and tear. Over the years, broken tiles had been replaced, but leaks were becoming increasingly challenging to prevent. The time had come for the clubhouse roof to undergo a much-needed replacement, ensuring its long-term durability and preserving its Spanish-style architectural charm.

Previous boards had long dreamed of making capital improvements and major repairs, but limited revenue prevented those dreams from materializing. However, we now had the opportunity to turn those dreams into action. During the May board meeting, the capital improvements committee presented a prioritized list of projects. Surprisingly, an irrigation system ranked among the lowest priorities, with even the golf committee chairman agreeing that it was unnecessary at this time. Despite being past chairman of the committee and recently reassigned to it, he had confidently assured the membership in the October 1987 meeting that he could grow grass without a new irrigation system. We jokingly suggested that if he could grow grass without water, he should sell the idea in Saudi Arabia.

Despite resilient common Bermuda grass fairways and a driving range acting as a Bermuda nursery, our course faced a tough previous year due to a severe drought. As spring turned into summer in 1988, we hoped for a normal season to revive our fairways. However, another summer-long drought hit unexpectedly, parching our fairways into a barren landscape by mid-July. During the Men's Invitational Tournament, we found ourselves playing on "286 red clay", a phrase coined by member Don Burton. He emphasized that even clay should have a number like grass does since we were on a golf course.

In the face of these challenges, we remained hopeful and convened a special board meeting four days after the tournament to discuss installing an irrigation system. Surprisingly, those who previously considered it a low-priority improvement changed their stance. With consecutive years of drought, a healthy financial condition, and a full membership, we embarked on the ambitious project of transforming our golf course into one of the finest in the area with a complete irrigation system, unanimously supported by the board.

The golf course chairman was given the responsibility of overseeing the irrigation project. The implementation faced some shortcomings due to insufficient planning and the rush to begin immediately. Instead of backfilling the trenches as the pipe was being laid, they continued to line our fairways, one after another. It appeared that the contractor's focus was on installing all the piping required before backfilling the trenches.

Most of the trenches did receive initial backfilling before the winter, but unfortunately, some did not receive any backfill, and by spring, additional backfilling was needed. As a result, some sprinkler heads were sunken deeper than necessary, and the riser pipes were not perfectly perpendicular. The original design also overlooked watering the rough in many areas, leading to undesirable conditions and necessitating a second irrigation system only 14 years later, highlighting the need for better planning. Nonetheless, the initial irrigation system effectively watered the fairways and automated the watering of the greens. We no longer had to endure playing on "286 red clay".

Chapter 15
CONTROVERSIAL ELECTIONS

The October quarterly board meeting in 1988 approached, coinciding with the election of three board members. This marked the third round of elections for the 12 board members chosen by the membership.

In the August board meeting preceding the election, three unelected directors from the previous administration were identified as having expiring terms and were eligible for election. Notably, for the first time since the membership began electing directors, one of these directors, specifically the director of the golf course committee, decided to run for re-election. Widely known and highly regarded by many members, his active involvement in the ongoing installation of our first irrigation system bolstered his candidacy.

The club's secretary, who was tasked with chairing the nominating/election committee, unfortunately failed to comply with the by-laws by not posting the nominees in the clubhouse ten days prior to the election. When the incumbent director failed to get re-elected, he filed a protest to the board, citing the deficiencies of the nominating committee. A special board meeting was called two days after the election to determine whether the election should be ratified. The President called the meeting to order and presented the protest. Several board members expressed their opinions, with a slight majority leaning towards not ratifying the election and holding a new one. The chairman of the nominating committee spoke and acknowledged the mistake but emphasized that it was unintentional.

As is my usual practice, I waited to hear others' thoughts before speaking. When I had the floor, I began by stating that there was no doubt that the by-law had not been followed. Therefore, the question at hand was whether the election was fair for all parties, and if so, it should be ratified. After a vote, the election was ratified. I then took the floor once again and suggested that the President establish a committee to draft instructions for future nominating committees, providing them with guidance on proper operations. The President asked, and I agreed to chair this committee, and by the next board meeting, we had a written set of instructions for the nominating committee. It was approved and used by future nominating chairpersons for several years. Unfortunately, over time, like many other approved board motions, it got lost and is no longer in use.

A year later, the director who had previously lost re-election made a comeback and was successfully elected for a four-year term. You may recall that three directors, known as officers, were not elected by the membership but rather by the board on an annual basis. It may seem rather peculiar, but the previous regime, during the property acquisition, had concerns about the possibility of one or more of the officers not being re-elected by the membership. This was their way of safeguarding against that scenario. Each year, during the March board meeting, the officers would stand for election by the board. If any officer failed to secure the majority of votes, they would be removed from their position. Since these officers were not elected by the membership, they would no longer serve as directors. Unfortunately, this created a potential problem. If the President or any other officer did not receive the majority of votes, they would no longer hold a position on the board and would be immediately replaced. In 1990, this exact situation unfolded.

During the March board meeting in 1990, a vote was conducted, but the President did not receive the necessary votes. Frustrated, he closed his binder and left the club. The former regime's attempt to protect the officers had backfired, resulting in an embarrassing moment. The secretary was promptly elected as the new President, and a discussion commenced regarding amending the by-laws to prevent a recurrence of this incident. I was asked and accepted the responsibility of chairing a by-laws committee tasked with rewriting the existing by-laws. I promptly assembled a committee consisting of two directors and three non-director members. We thoroughly examined all the by-laws, and by the October meeting, they had been approved by the board and presented to the membership for their ratification.

Interestingly, October marked the end of my term as a director, and I made the decision not to seek re-election. I had accomplished everything I had set out to do when I ran in 1987, and the fact that I never truly desired the position made my choice straightforward and effortless. Looking back, I am proud of the contributions I made to the club during my tenure as a director, and I am grateful for the opportunity to have served alongside dedicated individuals who shared a common vision for the club's success.

Chapter 16
POST-BOARD MEMBER YEARS

A new President assumed office in November of 1992, bringing new ideas, a fresh perspective, and a commitment to improving the overall experience of our members. The newly implemented by-laws mandated the President to appoint a nominating committee for a one-year term during the November board meeting, ensuring a fair and transparent process for selecting candidates. The committee was to consist of one director and two members, and I was honored to be appointed as one of the members.

In March, one of the directors resigned, creating a vacancy that needed to be filled. This necessitated a special election at the July board meeting to elect a suitable candidate to serve the remaining term. Instead of relying solely on members to self-nominate, as previous committees had done, we took a proactive approach by actively seeking out the most qualified candidates within the club. Each committee member was provided with a comprehensive membership list and tasked with identifying potential candidates of their choice, considering their expertise, dedication, and passion for the well-being of the club. Following this, committee members reached out to these candidates to gauge their willingness to run for office and contribute to the club's growth.

As committee members gathered to discuss the potential nominees, we were pleased to discover the rich talent of our membership. It was an opportunity for our club's diverse membership to shine as we plunged into the qualifications and potential of each candidate. The club's by-laws ensured transparency by requiring the names of candidates to be posted in the clubhouse and published in the monthly newsletter, allowing members to familiarize themselves with the candidates.

It was fascinating to see how individuals who might have been overlooked initially emerged as strong contenders once we had a comprehensive list for review. Taking a proactive approach, we nominated five candidates, exceeding the minimum required number. This guaranteed that the club had a rich pool of talent to draw from, strengthening its leadership and vision.

Following the election, I received unexpected news from the President: I was being removed from the nominations committee. While I didn't question the reason for his decision, I suspected it might be related to my involvement in another committee. I firmly believed the President lacked the authority to remove me, as the by- laws clearly stated that nomination committee appointments were for a one-year term. I respectfully conveyed this to the President, emphasizing the importance of adhering to established rules and processes. He responded by highlighting that the board had the final say in interpreting the by-laws, and I wished him luck in convincing the board of his perspective.

In addition to the nominations committee, I served on a committee discussing the construction of new golf cart paths. During our deliberations, we sought expert input from a club member who was a designer at a multi-state engineering firm located in Paducah so we could make an informed decision. However, despite careful consideration, we reached a deadlock over whether to use asphalt or concrete for the paths.

When the President who was observing our meeting sought to cast a vote, I respectfully reminded him that according to the by- laws, he didn't have a role in our committee's decision-making process. This established the importance of adhering to established rules and maintaining fairness within the club.

With the committee deadlocked, our only choice was to present our findings to the board without a specific recommendation. This allowed the board to weigh the options based on the information provided, ultimately choosing asphalt despite the President's apparent dissatisfaction.

These experiences highlighted the importance of following by-laws, transparency, and valuing diverse perspectives within our club. While challenges arose, it was through open dialogue and a commitment to established processes that the best decisions emerged, safeguarding the well-being of our membership and the club as a whole.

Chapter 17
NEW GREENS

In 1988, the installation of an irrigation system breathed new life into the Bermuda fairways of our golf course, restoring them to their former glory as some of the finest in Western Kentucky. As the fairways regained their lush appearance, they also became more playable, drawing golfers from near and far.

While the irrigation system brought improvement to the Bermuda greens, it became clear that their overall health was hindered by the lack of a proper drainage system. Several greens required a complete rebuild to ensure their long-term sustainability and optimal playing conditions, leading to a gradual reconstruction process starting in 1993.

The reconstruction efforts focused initially on holes 9, 13, and 16, where new greens were installed with state-of-the-art drainage systems in accordance with USGA specifications. The goal was to create greens that not only met the highest standards of playability but also ensured proper water drainage, preventing any damage because of stagnant waterlogged surfaces.

While the overall reconstruction process was undertaken with good intentions, it faced some challenges along the way. Due to inadequate planning, the rebuild fell short of perfection, leaving room for further improvements. The 13th Green emerged as the most successful of the three. Positioned on a hillside with a steep slope from back to front and right to left, the redesign mitigated the severity of the slope, subtly adjusting its positioning and contours to create a fair challenge for golfers.

However, not all greens turned out as expected. The 9th green unintentionally ended up with a small mound resembling an elephant burial site, adding a unique and whimsical element to the course. The 16th Green underwent a significant transformation, becoming a two-tier green that added an extra layer of challenge to the hole. Unfortunately, the transition between the lower and upper tiers proved to be particularly demanding, with an abnormally challenging transition that ultimately needed to be addressed later.

Following the subsequent yearly election of directors, the three newly elected board members aligned with others on the board who recognized the need for a complete overhaul of the golf course and significant renovations to the clubhouse.

By 1995, concrete plans were taking shape, with the election of three more like-minded directors paving the way for progress. Under the leadership of the newly elected President, Greg Nichols, a comprehensive plan was developed to revitalize the entire golf course. The services of golf course architect Jerry Lemmons from Nashville, Tennessee, were secured to lend his expertise and help bring the vision to life. A dedicated committee was formed, multiple meetings were held with the architect, plans for the clubhouse renovation were being finalized, and Greg had arranged the necessary financing with a local bank.

One of the challenges faced during this process was persuading the membership to embrace bent grass for the greens, replacing the Bermuda grass that had been used since 1926. Bent grass is known for its superior playing surface, its ability to hold an approach shot, and its ability to be played year-round.

With each step, the golf course's transformation was becoming more tangible and promising. The dedication and collaboration of the board, the expertise of the architect, and the support of the membership were all instrumental in shaping the golf course into a modern and exceptional facility that would be cherished by golfers for years to come.

The Country Club of Paducah, renowned for its exclusivity and prestige, made a significant addition to its offerings in 1981. Under the expert guidance of renowned golf course architect Robert Trent Jones, the club constructed a brand new 18-hole course that would soon garner nationwide recognition. With meticulously designed bent greens, the course provided an unparalleled playing experience for its esteemed members.

Initially, the Country Club of Paducah catered exclusively to a select group of elite professionals, including doctors, lawyers, bank officers, and business owners. However, when the club relocated to its new course on the outskirts of Paducah, some of the older members opted not to make the longer journey, resulting in a need to attract new members. To address this, the club took an innovative approach by reducing its initiation fee to an enticing $1000.00, opening its doors to a fresh wave of mid-level professionals seeking to join its prestigious ranks.

The new course quickly established itself as one of the top 100 in the country, thanks to its impeccable design and the unmatched beauty of its surroundings. Yet, despite the club's larger golf course budget compared to its counterpart, Rolling Hills, the Country Club of Paducah faced some unexpected challenges. Starting in 1987, specific greens on the course began experiencing issues each year, causing concerns among the members and the management alike.

Naturally, members of Rolling Hills were hesitant about transitioning to bent greens. However, there were numerous advantages to consider: improved putting surfaces, better holding surfaces for approach shots, and the ability to play on them year-round. With Bermuda greens, the club had to cover them with straw in November and use temporary greens until March. Unfortunately, that wasn't all. The regular greens were only in pristine condition for three months out of the year. Since Bermuda thrives in hot and humid conditions, it wasn't until June that our greens were perfect. In March, the straw was either raked or burned, leaving us with bare greens to play on. In April, the Bermuda grass started growing, resulting in semi-bare greens. In May, the greens would be top- dressed to promote Bermuda growth. In September, the greens were aerated and top-dressed to prepare them for winter. By then, the Bermuda was semi-dormant, preventing full recovery. Thus, we played on six different putting surfaces throughout the year: March, April, May, summer, fall, and winter greens.

By the time the crucial August board meeting of 1996 arrived, Greg, our President, was prepared to present the membership with the renovation plan for our golf course and clubhouse. The anticipation among the members was palpable, as prior notice had been sent to alert them about the upcoming presentation. Approximately 100 members attended the meeting, eager to hear the details of the proposed changes.

One of the main concerns voiced by the attendees was how the club could successfully maintain bent greens when the Country Club of Paducah faced challenges in doing so. Jerry Lemons, the architect for the golf course, was invited to deliver a detailed presentation and address these concerns. He explained that the struggles of CC of Paducah could be attributed to two primary factors. First, the greens had been constructed according to Robert Trent Jones' specifications, which slightly differed from the USGA specifications that he would implement for our greens. Second, in their pursuit of an exceptionally fast putting speed during the summer, CC of Paducah had been cutting the grass unusually low.

However, Jerry assured the members that bent grass greens could still achieve the desired speed without requiring such extreme measures. All that is needed is a light top-dressing once a week, the type that would go unnoticed the following day.

The proposal to switch to bent greens faced opposition from some vocal members, particularly the older ones who were resistant to change. As I observed from the audience that evening, it felt like an initial reading of the proposal that would likely fail but would help condition the membership for a future successful attempt. Unbeknownst to me, Greg already had the board's support to pass the proposal and was simply appeasing the membership. After extensive discussion, including one member threatening to resign if the plan proceeded, a vote was called, and the proposal was approved. This marked the beginning of our journey to become the second-best golf course in the area.

Chapter 18
A NEW GOLF COURSE

Following the successful August board meeting, we promptly proceeded to sign comprehensive contracts with the highly regarded and experienced Jerry Lemmons.

With his expertise and proficiency, Jerry took charge as both the architect and overseer of the ambitious renovation project for our esteemed golf course. The scope of the renovation encompassed various aspects, including the complete reshaping and construction of the greens to USGA specifications for seeding in bent grass, renovation of sand traps along with building new traps, the construction of new tee boxes along with the in-depth restoration of the existing ones, and the creation of some brand new fairways.

This transformative effort revitalized the course, breathing new life into its landscape with a detailed redesigned layout that now boasted a par 72, complete with an impressive new 4th par five 18th hole.

Not stopping there, we sought to enhance the overall golfing experience by introducing new amenities and facilities. A state-of-the-art driving range, practice greens, and a chipping area were carefully constructed to provide golfers with ample opportunities for polishing their skills and perfecting their game. These additions complemented the already exceptional course, ensuring a truly immersive and enjoyable golfing experience.

Simultaneously, our long-awaited plans to rejuvenate the clubhouse were set in motion. The main floor ballroom underwent a stunning transformation, featuring leveled and beautifully refinished hardwood floors. The ambiance of the main floor was elevated to new heights, adorned with freshly installed carpeting and a fresh coat of paint to the walls in soothing earth-tone colors, exuding a refreshing and inviting atmosphere. The open rafters were painstakingly cleaned, eliminating years of accumulated dust and restoring the grandeur of the space. To further enhance the elegance, we spared no expense in furnishing the ballroom and lounge with luxurious new tables and chairs, creating a sophisticated and comfortable setting for members and guests alike.

Recognizing the importance of comfort and convenience, we installed a state-of-the-art central heating and air conditioning system to ensure optimal temperature control throughout the clubhouse. Additionally, the pro shop was strategically relocated to optimize flow and better manage the needs of golfers, providing seamless access to equipment and expert advice.

Addressing the issue of rainwater leakage in the basement, a French drain was thoughtfully installed around the exterior perimeter of the walk-out basement, effectively resolving any potential concerns. To maximize the breathtaking views, a stunning concrete deck was added at the back of the clubhouse, offering a picturesque vantage point overlooking the swimming pool, tennis courts, and the majestic 12th green. This addition provided members and guests with a tranquil and scenic spot to relax and appreciate the natural beauty that surrounds our esteemed club.

Last but certainly not least, we created a new staging area for golfers, meticulously designed to streamline the flow and enhance the overall golfing experience. Also, a new scoreboard was installed in this area, ensuring that important updates and information would be readily available to all players and spectators.

In May 1997, with great pride and excitement, we unveiled the remarkable transformation of our golf course, achieving what once seemed unimaginable just a few short years prior. Over the next eight years, our dedicated efforts and commitment to excellence allowed us to successfully maintain the pristine bent grass greens without any major issues despite having multiple greens superintendents come and go. Rolling Hills Golf Club flourished, attracting a diverse membership from all walks of life and radiating an atmosphere of excitement, vibrancy, and camaraderie.

The irrigation system, originally installed in 1988, served its purpose well over the years. However, by 2001, a small group of forward-thinking members felt it was time for an upgrade. The main issue with the original system was its single-line design, which provided inadequate coverage outside the fairway. This limitation made it challenging to maintain a lush rough, impeding our ability to offer a truly exceptional golfing experience. While we were proud of our Bermuda fairways, which were among the best in the four-state area, new members and their fresh perspectives highlighted the need for improvement. Thus, a movement began to develop, advocating for a dual-line irrigation system that would address these issues once and for all.

In 2001, the board, recognizing the importance of delivering unparalleled quality to our members, voted in favor of this ambitious endeavor. Once again, we entrusted the expertise of Jerry Lemmons to design and oversee the installation of an innovative and comprehensive irrigation system that would revolutionize our course maintenance practices. With his guidance, the installation of the new irrigation system was executed seamlessly, and the results were truly remarkable. Our roughs began to flourish, becoming lush and vibrant, further enhancing the overall beauty and playability of the course.

During that period, our membership remained optimal, and our financial standing was solid. This gave us the confidence to pursue the funds needed for the project and restructure our debt, ensuring the feasibility of this significant endeavor. However, it was important to maintain our current membership level to mitigate any potential setbacks from a decline in membership. The successful completion of the new irrigation system installation marked another milestone in our ongoing commitment to providing an exceptional golfing experience for our cherished members.

Looking back on the remarkable journey that brought us here, we take immense pride in the progress and accomplishments we've achieved. Rolling Hills Country Club has not only become a premier destination for golf enthusiasts but has also evolved into a vibrant community that exudes belonging and brotherhood among its diverse members. With each passing year, our dedication to excellence and continuous improvement remains steadfast, ensuring that Rolling Hills Country Club will thrive and provide unforgettable experiences for years to come.

Chapter 19
SOCIAL ACTIVITIES

Rolling Hills' social events were always filled with enthusiasm and excitement. Throughout the year, we had a wide variety of dances scheduled, each with its own unique theme to create a magical atmosphere. From the enchanting Valentine's dance, where couples swayed to romantic melodies, to the thrilling Halloween dance, filled with costumes and spooky decorations, there was something for everyone to enjoy.

One of the most memorable dances was the 50's/60's themed night, taking everyone back in time to the era of rock and roll and vibrant fashion. The dance floor was filled with groovy moves and retro outfits, transporting everyone to a nostalgic and energetic atmosphere. And, of course, we always held a dance contest featuring the iconic dances of the era: Jitterbug, Cha-Cha-Cha, The Twist, Hand Jive, Bunny Hop, Monkey, Swim, Mash Potato, and my personal favorite, The East Coast Swing.

As the year came to a close, the New Year's Eve dance was the grand finale of the social calendar. It was a night of glitz and glamour, with sparkling decorations, elegant attire, and a countdown to welcome the new year. The dance floor was alive with joy and anticipation as everyone celebrated the beginning of a fresh chapter.

Since its inception, the bar has always been a focal point of social events since we did not have a restaurant. The clubhouse and bar were open until 10 pm Sunday through Wednesday and extended to 1 am on Thursday through Saturday. Thursday was designated as Men's Day, from 12 pm until closing, exclusively for the golf course and the bar. For a modest price of $6, steaks were available to cook on a charcoal grill, accompanied by a baked potato and salad. Over the years, the price gradually increased, but even today, it remains at a modest $17.

Every Tuesday, Ladies' Day was the highlight, running from 10 am to 4 pm. In 1987, a night ladies' league was introduced, starting with a shotgun format on one of the 9-hole sides. In the sunroom, a card game of gin could be found during most afternoons, and on Saturdays, it continued throughout the day. Friday evenings during the summer attracted a significant crowd for couples golf, featuring 3-couple teams playing a 9-hole scramble format. Participants had the option to organize their own team or sign up as a single couple and be assigned a team, which proved to be an excellent way for new couples to be introduced and make new friends. After golf, most couples would either dine out or have pizza delivered to the club.

Rolling Hills was undeniably a vibrant destination, with numerous members flocking to the bar until the late hours of Friday nights. In the winter of 2001, I proposed the idea of having our own music entertainment by spinning our own records, or rather CDs, at that time. I provided the use of an amplifier, mixer, CD players, and speakers. The concept gained popularity, and The Club even agreed to invest in their own equipment. For several years, during the winter months, it became a beloved tradition on Friday nights, bridging the gap between different generations of members. Members created their own custom CDs and took turns performing disc jockey duties.

Steve Bauer, a fairly new member at the time, became so passionate about it that he purchased his own equipment, not only for DJing but also for providing Karaoke, which he still does occasionally to this day. However, Friday nights never quite matched the level of support achieved on Men's Night, which remained the epitome of attendance by the men of Rolling Hills. One notable change over the past 20 years has been the decline in member participation at the club after 9 pm.

THE CLUB

The atmosphere at Rolling Hills was always buzzing with anticipation as members eagerly awaited the start of each event. From the sizzling aroma of steaks grilling on the charcoal grill during Men's Day to the cheerful laughter of couples participating in the 9-hole scramble format on Fridays, the club was a hub of energy and camaraderie. As the sun set and the stars adorned the sky, the bar became a lively gathering spot, with members sharing stories, laughter, and creating lasting memories.

Over the years, Rolling Hills Country Club has embraced innovation to cater to its members' diverse interests. Initiatives like Ladies' Day and the Night Ladies' League provide female members with opportunities to showcase their golfing skills and form connections with like-minded individuals. Meanwhile, the sunroom became a hub for friendly gin competitions, strengthening the bond between members.

Friday evenings in the summer saw couples hitting the links together, strengthening their bonds as they navigated the course and celebrated their successes. The addition of music entertainment on these nights brought a new level of excitement, with members taking turns as DJs and creating a lively atmosphere with various musical genres. Karaoke nights, organized by passionate members, added yet another layer of fun and laughter to the club's social gatherings.

Despite changes in member participation patterns, Rolling Hills remained committed to providing a welcoming and enjoyable experience for all. While late-night attendance declined, the spirit of togetherness and shared passion for the club's offerings endured. As the club continued to adapt and innovate, it held onto the tradition of excitement and cherished memories lived on for generations.

Chapter 20
CONTROVERSIAL BOARD DECISION

Board members come and go, and when they are elected solely based on popularity, it can lead to dire consequences. However, if the nominating committee fulfills its responsibilities diligently, the chances of electing the most qualified individuals as board members greatly increase. Unfortunately, not all nominating committees took their role seriously, and for several years, starting in 2000, we ended up with board members who were not the most qualified.

In 2002, a newly elected board member had an agenda that disrupted the order of who had the first right to play in the Men's Member Guest Tournament. This tournament, initiated by the Men's Golf Association in 1987, has been the highlight event at our club since its inception. The tournament always had a full field with a waiting list, and it could take several years for someone on the waiting list to secure a spot. Previously, those who played in the previous year had until a specific date to sign up for the current year's tournament. After that date, individuals on the waiting list would have a chance, followed by others. However, this new board member proposed a change to this process, suggesting that those on the waiting list should have first rights to play. To my surprise, and the majority of the membership, the board approved this change. Naturally, the membership expressed their dissatisfaction, leading to the necessity of a special board meeting.

As one can imagine, the meeting was quite hostile. I attended and took the opportunity to address the board, expressing my concern about the new decision. I likened it to giving priority to those on the waiting list for a cart shed, forcing current shed owners to vacate until everyone on the list was accommodated. The board member who introduced the policy immediately objected, stating that my argument was absurd. In response, I replied, "Sometimes, you have to be absurd to show absurdity."

Our golf pro, Kevin Rhinehart, then took the floor and proposed a solution to the problem. He suggested implementing a shotgun start with morning and afternoon sessions for the tournament, ensuring that all interested players could participate, but this would close the course for other members to play. The board agreed to this idea, effectively resolving the issue. However, this decision did mean that the course would be closed to members who did not participate in the tournament, which was precisely what previous boards had tried to avoid.

Chapter 21
THE DISASTER

Since its complete rebuild in 1996, our beloved golf course has continuously undergone improvements to ensure an exceptional experience for all golf enthusiasts. One notable enhancement was the implementation of a state-of-the-art dual-line irrigation system, which has significantly benefited the areas surrounding the fairways. This ambitious project, spanning over the past two years, has successfully transformed these areas into lush green spaces that perfectly complement the course's natural beauty.

To further elevate the overall quality of our course, we made a conscious decision to invest in the growth and maintenance of fescue grass in our roughs. While this decision has undeniably added to the budget of the golf course, we firmly believe that the extra time and effort dedicated to ensuring the fescue grass is at the ideal length provides golfers with an unforgettable experience. The sight of perfectly manicured roughs not only adds visual appeal but also serves as a testament to our commitment to excellence.

In late 2004, a new golf course superintendent joined our team, and the summer of 2005 presented an opportunity for him to showcase his exceptional skills in maintaining and enhancing our golf course. One area that immediately caught our attention was the wooded area between holes #1 and #9, which also serves as the entrance to our prestigious clubhouse. Previous superintendents had neglected this area, leading us to believe that growing grass here was an impossible feat. However, to our astonishment, our newly appointed superintendent effortlessly brought life to this once- neglected area with his remarkable talent for growing grass in challenging environments.

As the summer progressed, little did we know that a devastating disaster was about to unfold. By the end of July, several of our greens were completely lost, and numerous others were plagued by extensive dead spots covering over 50% of their surface. It was a disheartening sight that left us in disbelief. One late afternoon in August, while standing on the ninth tee, I couldn't help but notice the abundance of grass thriving in the woods between holes 9 and 1. In a lighthearted jest, I jokingly remarked, "Well, it seems that David can grow grass everywhere except on the greens!" Little did I know that this seemingly innocent comment marked the beginning of a challenging period for our club's viability.

With swift action, the board directed David, our superintendent, to prepare for reseeding the greens and thoroughly investigate the root cause of the disaster. To ensure accuracy, we brought in an expert from the Kentucky Golf Association, a USGA affiliate, to consult and take core samples. The results revealed a layer of thatch, approximately 1" below the surface, as the culprit. This issue had been brewing over several years of neglect, predating David's tenure. Understanding the challenge he inherited, the board granted him leeway.

Further investigation uncovered that the type of sand used for top dressing was suboptimal, likely exacerbating the problem. Following the KGA's advice, we procured a silo to store sand, ensuring it remained dry and readily available. With the greens reseeding and cooler temperatures in September, they gradually regained their pristine condition, erasing the bitter memory of the disaster. However, another twist awaited us.

Spring 2006 promised an exciting golf season at Rolling Hills Golf Club, nestled among picturesque landscapes. Although our bent grass greens allowed year-round play, most golfers preferred a break during winter, eagerly awaiting March to resume play. Throughout the summer, we hosted three major tournaments: The Duke and Duchess,

The Men's Invitational, and The Men's Member Guest, each meticulously scheduled for optimal weather.

However, the hot, humid conditions of summer posed a threat to our delicate bent greens if not properly maintained. Despite believing the previous disaster was a one-time occurrence, we faced a devastating reality a few days after the Men's Invitational Tournament in July. Once again, we found ourselves losing our greens, leaving the board and membership perplexed and disheartened. We had believed the problem was solved, but evidently, it persisted.

After the Men's Member Guest Tournament in August, reseeding once again was the norm. Coupled with the cooler temperatures that September brings, we were finally able to witness a glimmer of hope as the greens began to recover. In an effort to prevent our greens from this devastating disaster in future years, various ideas were proposed and passionately debated. Suggestions ranged from cooling the greens with permanent fans, clearing more trees to improve airflow, renting specialized equipment for extra deep tine aeration and top dressing, and raising the mower height to give the grass blades a better chance of survival.

Unfortunately, despite our best efforts, the club began to experience a decline in membership, particularly among those who had no financial stake due to membership drives that offered waived initiation fees. By the end of 2006, our once-thriving membership had fallen well below 500 for the first time since reaching this level in 1988. It was a challenging period for our club as we grappled with the consequences of the recurring greens issue and its impact on our membership.

The following year, an air of apprehension loomed as the Men's tournament in July approached. Would the greens miraculously survive long enough to provide the exceptional golf course conditions we all longed for? And would they remain resilient throughout the rest of the summer?

As everyone held their breath and hoped for a miracle, we were granted a much-needed reprieve. Our greens not only survived the tournament but also thrived without any issues. A collective sigh of relief swept through the membership, and it seemed that the worst was finally behind us.

However, fate had a different plan in store for us the following year. With mixed emotions of anticipation and anxiety, we faced yet another disaster, with the greens once again needing to be reseeded. By now, our greens superintendent had become an expert in reseeding greens, and once again, the greens recovered by November.

Over the next two years, we experienced the loss of greens in 2009 but managed to avoid it in 2010, marking a period of both relief and cautious optimism. Throughout the span of seven long years, we endured the loss of our greens for five of those years, a reality that was not a favorable reflection on our greens superintendent.

Nonetheless, as a resilient club, we continued to persevere with the same superintendent, hoping for better results with our greens. You've likely heard the age-old saying, *"The definition of insanity is doing the same thing over and over again, expecting a different outcome."* Well, we found ourselves trapped in the clutches of that very saying!

Chapter 22
ANOTHER FINANCIAL CRISIS

As we started losing members due to the greens issue, another financial crisis emerged. It all began when a newly elected Treasurer took it upon himself to implement QuickBooks for our bookkeeping needs and financial statements. Apparently, due to unforeseen circumstances, the QuickBooks implementation was never fully completed, leading to significant gaps in our financial management. This issue went unnoticed until 2011, when I became treasurer and restructured and fully implemented the use of QuickBooks.

It is, however, important to note that the QuickBooks mishap was not the sole reason for our financial troubles. The root of the problem actually started a few years earlier with the acquisition and financing of the dual-line irrigation system. Coupled with the additional expense of reseeding the greens in 2005 and 2006, as well as the consecutive loss of membership due to the greens issue, our financial well-being was severely strained.

To safeguard against unforeseen circumstances, we have maintained a line of credit of $150,000 since the renovation in 1997. This line of credit was intended for emergencies only, and it remained unused until the newly elected treasurer started using it to cover normal operating expenses without fully understanding its purpose.

At the time, the board either failed to pay attention or lacked the financial acumen to comprehend the monthly financial reports. As a result, no alarms were raised when the line of credit was being utilized, accumulating additional debt each month. Throughout the year, the board proposed new projects, and each time, they asked the treasurer if we had the necessary funds. The response was always affirmative, further contributing to the financial strain.

One such project involved replacing the deteriorating double doors at the main entrance to the clubhouse. Although the original solid wooden arched doors had been functioning adequately since the clubhouse was built in 1926, age had taken its toll. Since we thought we had surplus funds, it made sense to replace them. The cost, though seemingly high at $8000, was approved by the board, and the new doors were installed.

As the door payment depleted our line of credit, the treasurer finally informed the board of the dire financial situation. The board met this news with displeasure, and the treasurer's explanation was that he believed the line of credit was meant to cover expenses. Subsequently, the treasurer resigned, and rumors of possible embezzlement circulated. However, despite their responsibility to review and approve the treasurer's financial reports each month, the board absolved themselves of any responsibility.

To investigate any potential embezzlement, a committee was formed consisting of two former treasurers and a past board member who had served as the president of a local bank. After several months of scrutiny, no evidence of embezzlement was found. The former treasurer had resigned from the club, and it was now imperative for us to tighten our financial belt. Consequently, for the next few years, only a limited number of improvements could be made to the club as we focused on stabilizing our financial situation and rebuilding our reserves.

Paul Holland, a former board member and treasurer, ran for the board in 2006 and was elected not only to the board but also as the new treasurer. Paul, an ultra-conservative with a keen eye for financial management, successfully implemented necessary financial restraints on the board, leading to a significant rebound in our financial condition over the next three years. His expertise and dedication paved the way for a more stable and prosperous future for our club.

However, as plans for interior improvements to the clubhouse, such as painting and new carpet, were starting to develop in the spring of 2010, a self-inflicted problem arose. Our Olympic-size swimming pool, originally constructed in 1926, had undergone renovations over the years to ensure it remained a centerpiece of our family-oriented club.

Some accounts suggested that the pool's walls were initially wooden, but there is no concrete evidence to support this claim. Rolling Hills Country Club, which began in 1956, had always boasted a sturdy and reliable concrete pool structure. In the 1970s, a new 4" concrete floor was installed; in 1989, a new liner was installed, and pressure relief valves were added to the deep end. A modern filtering system was implemented in the early 70s. Prior to having a filtering system, the pool was drained every Sunday evening and refilled on Monday.

In 2010, a newly elected board member took charge as the chairman of the pool committee. Without fully investigating how previous committees had operated, he proactively contacted the health department to inquire about the requirements for opening the pool. Unfortunately, this well-intentioned action led to unforeseen consequences. The health department inspected the situation and concluded that, despite enjoying grandfather status for our existing pool in the past, this exemption was no longer applicable. We now faced a daunting choice: either finance and construct a brand-new pool or consider the heartbreaking possibility of closing it altogether.

After several meetings with the health department and other officials, a solution emerged. They allowed us to open the pool for 2010 on the condition that we commit to replacing it by 2011. With a sense of urgency and determination, a dedicated committee for the construction of a new swimming pool was formed. They sought the guidance of a reputable pool contractor from Louisville, Kentucky, to develop plans that would balance the cost-effectiveness and the grandeur of our swimming pool. After careful consideration, it was determined that constructing a replacement pool on the inside of the existing pool would be the most feasible approach. This decision not only minimized costs but also eliminated the need to demolish the existing pool. We sought a loan from the bank to finance the construction and imposed a $20 per month debt assessment on the members over a five-year period to repay the incurred debt.

The construction of the new pool proceeded smoothly, adhering to the schedule, and our members eagerly awaited its grand opening. Finally, on Memorial Weekend 2011, our new pool welcomed members and guests, ready to embrace them with open arms. With its updated design and contemporary amenities, it transformed into an even more enticing space for relaxation, recreation, and the birth of cherished memories.

The path to this milestone wasn't devoid of challenges, but the resilience and unity within our club prevailed. As a result, we unveiled a new pool that not only represents our commitment to progress but also embodies the enduring spirit of Rolling Hills.

Chapter 23
THE TOBACCO CONTROVERSY

There are still several members who strongly oppose the idea of making our facility a Tobacco-free environment. They argue that smoking is a legal activity for those over 18 and believe that individuals should have the freedom to choose whether or not to smoke. But, it is important to note that tobacco use is not only a personal health risk but also a public health concern. It is the leading cause of premature morbidity and mortality worldwide, affecting not only the smokers themselves but also those exposed to secondhand smoke.

Numerous studies have demonstrated the detrimental effects of secondhand smoke, suggesting that there is no safe level of exposure. This has led to an increasing number of people advocating for the elimination of smoking in public places. The decision to make our club tobacco-free was not an easy one, as it sparked a divide among members and even influenced board elections.

Back in 2007, the board approved a referendum to vote on whether our club should become tobacco-free. Unfortunately, it was narrowly defeated, reflecting the differing opinions within our membership. In 2009, during the board elections, some candidates campaigned against making our club tobacco-free, and one of them eventually became the president. His stance on allowing smoking as long as he held the position caused further tension among members.

As the August 2010 board meeting approached, my brother-in-law, who was a board member, sought my advice on how to bring up the issue of a tobacco-free policy for discussion. His friends had been urging him to address this before his tenure ended on November 1st.

I advised him on the strategic approach of making a motion during the new business portion of the meeting, ensuring that another board member was ready to second the motion. This tactical move aimed to limit the opposition's options, forcing them to either table or postpone the motion.

Due to the majority of board members' unfamiliarity with "Robert's Rules of Order," I attended the meeting to prevent the president from using inappropriate tactics to suppress the movement. Normally, our board meetings were quite informal, with discussions taking place even when no motions were in order. The president argued that the motion was out of order because it was not on the agenda, but I interjected by citing "Robert's Rules of Order," which states that new business is there for items that are not on the agenda.

Since the motion was properly made and seconded, and no motion to table or postpone was introduced, it had to be considered by the board. After 15 minutes of discussion, a vote was called, and the motion passed by a margin of one vote!

Enraged, the president closed his notebook and abruptly announced his resignation from the board. His impulsive action likely sealed the fate of smoking at the club. With the imminent yearly election of three board members, all of whom supported a tobacco-free club, the president only required the election of one member who favored smoking to reintroduce the motion. This time, the votes were likely to be in his favor, and as the president, he possessed the authority to cast the deciding vote in case of a tie. Thanks to his impulsive action, we have remained tobacco-free to this day.

This issue electrified the upcoming election in October. The smoking members were furious about the board's decision to make our campus tobacco-free, and they put forth several candidates for election. Additionally, two other groups in favor of maintaining a tobacco-free environment emerged with the intent to put forth their own candidates for the board. Normally, only three positions would be voted on, but due to the president's resignation, a fourth member would be included in this election. Recognizing that the two pro-tobacco-free groups might split the votes, allowing the possibility of smokers being elected, I contacted Nick Mills to arrange a meeting between both groups. Our goal was to select the best four candidates from our combined group.

We succeeded in our efforts, and during the November board meeting, a motion was made, seconded, and passed to implement a tobacco-free environment starting the following day! As we exited the board meeting, I engaged in a discussion with one of the board members who supported smoking at the club. For the first time, I learned why smokers were so frustrated. The club was their last refuge!

They were prohibited from smoking at work, in restaurants, and even at home, and now they were no longer allowed to smoke at their own club.

Following a highly contentious board decision, the already existing rift between club members deepened, sending shockwaves through the tight-knit community. One member, who had been an integral part of the club for over 25 years, was so consumed by fury and disappointment that he impulsively decided to sever ties with the club, abruptly quitting in a fit of anger. However, as time passed and the dust settled, he came to a profound realization: the club he had cherished for so long would never allow smoking again, a decision that had fueled his initial outrage. With a newfound sense of clarity, he chose to renew his membership, eager to once again be a part of the club he had called home for so many years.

Meanwhile, another member, who had enthusiastically booked the ballroom for a glamorous business Christmas party, found themselves in a predicament following the board's decision. Faced with the inevitable clash between their plans and the club's new smoking policy, they wasted no time in promptly canceling the reservation the very next day, unwilling to compromise their vision for the event.

Tensions within the club were further exacerbated when a few members engaged in a heated argument on Men's night later that week, adding fuel to the already simmering fire. The once harmonious atmosphere that had characterized the club was now overshadowed by palpable tension and discord.

On a chilly Friday night, as club members gathered to socialize and seek solace amidst the ongoing turmoil, I found myself immersed in a conversation with friends, reflecting on the canceled business Christmas party. At that moment, a spark of inspiration ignited within me, and a daring idea began to take shape in my mind. With steadfast resolve, I proposed to two of my closest friends that we should take matters into our own hands and rent the ballroom, hosting our own Christmas party for the club members we held dear. Excitement filled the air as five couples enthusiastically joined forces, eagerly embracing their roles as hosts for the much- anticipated event.

The intricately planned soirée promised an evening of enchantment, complete with an array of delectable hors d'oeuvres especially curated to tantalize the taste buds of the esteemed guests. Word of the upcoming celebration spread like wildfire, quickly becoming the talk of the season. As the night progressed, the ballroom pulsated with the captivating energy emanating from Steve Bauer Houndawg, the DJ extraordinaire. His delightful musical choices created an enchanting ambiance, setting the stage for an absolutely unforgettable experience that was hailed as the most anticipated and memorable party of the year.

Remarkably, even the members who had initially canceled the ballroom reservation found themselves unable to resist the allure of the festivities. Alongside them, the long-time member who had previously resigned, recognizing the undeniable sense of brotherhood and unity that pervaded the event, decided to attend.

In the heat of the swirling emotions and the tumultuous journey that had unfolded within the club, this magically reflected the indomitable spirit of its members. It was a celebration of unity, friendship, and the strong belief that even in the face of adversity, the bonds we create can overcome any obstacle.

The tobacco controversy at our club was a complex and heated issue that ultimately led to a significant decision. While it was met with opposition from some members, it also garnered support from those who recognized the importance of creating a healthier and smoke-free environment. The path to becoming tobacco-free was not easy, but the outcome has been a positive one for the overall well-being of Rolling Hills Country Club.

Chapter 24
THE LONG-AWAITED REMEDY

Memorial Weekend 2011 buzzed with excitement at Rolling Hills as we unveiled our pristine, brand-new swimming pool. Its sparkling water shimmered under the summer sun, beckoning members to plunge in and escape the impending heat of June, July, and August. Despite successfully nurturing our greens back to life in the previous year, there lingered a sense of apprehension about their survival in the long run.

Stepping into a new role on the board added another layer of responsibility to my plate. I had been elected to fill the term of a member who resigned in December, specifically with the aim of taking on the treasurer's duties. Our monthly board meetings, typically held on the second Monday, provided a platform for discussing club matters and making crucial decisions.

However, during a December meeting I attended, some board members rightly voiced concerns about the timing of financial reports. They questioned why these reports couldn't be distributed at least a week in advance, allowing for thorough review and preparation. The treasurer at the time deferred the question to Paul Holland, who, although no longer on the board, handled bookkeeping tasks for the club.

Paul's explanation puzzled me. He cited the delay in receiving bank statements as the reason for the tardy reports, despite our use of QuickBooks. Once I became treasurer, I discovered that our QuickBooks system was limited to tracking income and expenditures, essentially serving as a glorified check-writing tool.

I took on the responsibility of check writing and deposit entries to fully integrate the club with QuickBooks, ensuring seamless financial management. The plan was to eventually delegate these tasks back to Paul once the integration was complete, allowing for easy generation of financial and budget reports at any time. The unexpired term that I had been elected to serve would conclude on November 1 of the same year, giving me just ten months to accomplish this task unless I decided to run for re-election for another 3-year term. I found myself experiencing the same sentiment that I had in 1990 – I never aspired to be a board member, and I hoped that I could achieve this goal within the given timeframe.

As the election nominations approached, I realized that I still needed an additional two months to complete the budget side of QuickBooks. Despite this setback, I made the decision to put my name forward for re-election, demonstrating my dedication to the club's financial well-being even if it meant serving another three years. Yet, a sense of anxiety lingered within me due to a couple of incidents that I had been involved in at the club over the past five months.

The first incident unfolded as a heated argument with another member on a Sunday afternoon, escalating into an unfortunate physical altercation. Both the other member and I received admonishment letters from the President, warning of more severe consequences if we were involved in any further incidents. The second incident took place a couple of months later, involving a non-member late on a Friday night, resulting in regrettable punches being thrown. The following day, the President, who happened to be a personal friend, reached out to me to check on my well-being and discuss the incident. Taking full responsibility for my actions, I suggested that I be suspended from the club for 30 days.

Aware of the potential negative reaction to my re-election bid, I firmly believed that the positive contributions I had made to the club would outweigh my missteps. Unfortunately, the final election outcome was a devastating defeat, marking the end of my tenure on the board. This result stood in stark contrast to the exultation I experienced during my first election in 1987.

Nevertheless, I continued my work for another 15 days until my term expired. During this period, I diligently continued training a new employee we had already hired as a replacement for Paul. I provided detailed instructions on how to build the budget reports, which were only generated up through September. Before implementing QuickBooks, the budget reports were created as spreadsheets for the entire year, so all board members had copies of those. They would then receive a copy of the current month's budget generated from QuickBooks. Despite no longer being on the board, I remained a member of the club and made myself available to Lisa if she had any questions or needed guidance.

Through the grapevine, I heard that some board members accused me of omitting an insurance payment scheduled for November from the budget. But, no one ever approached me about this matter, leaving me unable to clarify the situation until now. The payment was included in the original year budget that I had meticulously created using the previous method of spreadsheets, and all board members had copies of it.

As I began building the monthly budget report to be generated by QuickBooks, I opted to generate each month's report as needed. The ultimate goal was to have a complete budget report by the end of the year, which could then be utilized in future years. So, I can only assume that instead of using the spreadsheet report, which included the November insurance liability, to generate the November budget report through QuickBooks, they used another method. Nevertheless, it is worth noting that the board members should have diligently reviewed both the year-long monthly report they received at the beginning of the year and the monthly report generated by QuickBooks. This would have allowed them to identify any discrepancy, including the omission of the November insurance liability.

Once again, our greens unexpectedly withered in July, leaving our club devastated. Board members immediately began exchanging emails, and I called John, our president, urging him to assemble a committee consisting of four board members and four non-board members. I also proposed that Matt Ihnen take on the role of committee chairman. John swiftly formed the committee, and I was honored to be selected as one of the board members to serve on it.

Matt and I agreed that one of our first steps should be to visit neighboring clubs with bent grass greens and consult with their greens superintendents. We wasted no time in arranging a meeting with Larry Hantle, the superintendent of The Country Club of Paducah, and within two days, we were engaged in a fruitful discussion.

I also reached out to Jerry Lemmons for his insights. Initially, I was concerned about potentially destroying evidence of the problem if we were to disturb the greens by re-seeding them. I wondered if our actions would obliterate any traces of what caused the issue. Should we have taken soil samples before intervening? Surprisingly, Jerry explained that the evidence lies in the maintenance procedures we employ for the greens. We participated in a lengthy conversation about proper bent grass green maintenance, and it became clear that our primary issue was our watering practices. This observation was reinforced during our discussion with Larry Hantle.

Matt and I spent approximately an hour and a half talking to Larry, during which the topic of watering emerged as the key factor in preserving bent greens. Larry recounted a conversation he had with a new board member assigned to the golf committee earlier this spring. The board member had asked Larry for a comprehensive watering schedule for the entire year. Larry's response was, "For the entire year? I don't have a schedule for the entire year! During the hot and humid months, I assess the conditions each morning and decide on that day's watering strategy!"

This revelation shed light on our own practices, which differed tremendously from Larry's. Larry even emphasized the importance of using a walk-behind mower instead of a rider for mowing bent greens.

Over the next few months, our committee visited various courses, gathering valuable information on the best maintenance practices to give our greens the best chance for survival. One member stumbled upon an article discussing bent greens in hot and humid conditions, citing research conducted by Kansas State University. The research concluded that "If you, as a greens superintendent, utilize an overhead irrigation system to water bent greens during hot and humid conditions, it's time to reconsider! The proper approach is to hand water until the water reaches the bottom of the roots and then refrain from watering until near-drought conditions. This means that you may need to hand water three or more times a day!" This was a game-changer, as it required discipline and commitment to properly care for bent greens.

Relying on the newfound knowledge we had acquired, we compiled a comprehensive report, which was shared with the board, the superintendent, and the membership. During my earlier conversation with Jerry Lemmons three months before, another intriguing revelation emerged.

Jerry mentioned that he had consulted for the past several years with a nine-hole course in the Nashville area that employed a retired farmer as their superintendent. This particular course faced no issues with its bent greens. I inquired about the possibility of Jerry consulting with Rolling Hills and the associated cost. This information was relayed to the committee, and Chairman Matt Ihnen continued the conversation with Jerry. By this time, my tenure as a board member had come to an end.

During a subsequent board meeting, Matt proposed a motion to hire Jerry Lemmons as a consultant for our bent greens. The annual cost was $10,000, and Jerry would visit our course multiple times between May and September to advise our superintendent on maintaining the greens. Considering the $20,000 expense of re-seeding the greens each year and the potential loss of membership due to subpar greens, this decision seemed obvious. But, concerns were raised about the lack of competitive bids. Unsure if there were other options available, Matt asked Jerry if he knew of any other consultants. Jerry recommended Mark Green, a recently retired superintendent from Valhalla Country Club in Louisville, KY, who had started his own consulting company.

Mark's fee matched Jerry's but included a guarantee that we would not owe anything if we lost any greens. As a result, the board decided to hire Mark Green for the consulting job. The years 2012 and 2013 proved exceptional, with flawless greens and no issues whatsoever. However, in 2014, our superintendent thought that Mark's visits were excessive, so the contract was slightly reduced with a further reduction in Mark's consulting, and we suffered devastating results. Once again, we lost our greens, and now the board had to consider replacing our superintendent.

During the August board meeting, many of the members attended to voice their opinions. I attended with the intention of presenting evidence of our superintendent's incompetence in the hope of ending his tenure. As the meeting began, the president announced that the golf course issue would be taken right away and allowed anyone who wanted to speak to be added to a list. Following my usual practice, I waited and listened to others express their opinions until someone suggested changing our greens to dwarf-type Bermuda grass.

With a quick raise of my hand and a nod from the chairman, I knew I was on the list to speak. While the discussion continued and I waited for my turn, our superintendent responded to the suggestion of changing the greens and asked me to speak on the subject since I had previously served on the greens committee. Mark Green, the consultant, was also present and had previously stated that David, our superintendent, had done nothing wrong and had followed all of his advice.

In response to David's remarks, I asked Mark if he had a copy of the report that our committee had compiled three years earlier and if he had read it. Mark replied, "I've never seen that report," while David admitted," I don't think I even have a copy of it." I began to share information from the report, citing the research conducted by Kansas State University on proper irrigation techniques for bent greens. "If you, as a greens superintendent, rely on an overhead irrigation system to water bent greens during hot and humid conditions, it's time to reconsider! The correct approach is to hand water until the water reaches the bottom of the roots and then refrain from watering until near-drought conditions. This means that you may need to hand-water three or more times a day!" Mark immediately interjected, pointing his finger at David, and exclaimed, "I've been telling him from day one that these greens need to be hand-watered!"

With that, the game was over. I felt that I had successfully presented evidence against David, and there was nothing more that needed to be said. The discussion continued for another 30 minutes until everyone had their say, and then the board took a recess before moving on to regular business. Later, they went into executive session to discuss David's future, and ultimately, his tenure came to an end on November 1st, 2016.

Chapter 25
THE SEARCH AND NEW BEGINNING

As soon as the decision was made to find a new superintendent, we wasted no time in starting the search. Led by Matt Ihnen, a trusted member of the committee, we set on the task with determination. Matt, serving as the committee chairman, carefully combed through the credentials of potential candidates, knowing full well the caliber of person we needed for the job.

Understanding the critical need for a superintendent experienced in maintaining bent greens within our region's transition zone – stretching from the northern point of Kentucky to the southern point of Tennessee – Matt sought advice from Jerry Lemmons, a seasoned expert whose guidance we valued immensely.

After an extensive search and careful review of multiple applicants, the committee narrowed down the pool of candidates to three highly qualified individuals. The interview process commenced, providing an opportunity to probe deeper into their experience, expertise, and overall suitability for the position. Among the candidates, Kraig emerged as the most qualified, possessing the right qualifications and experience, with the exception of direct experience in the transition zone.

Despite the lack of specific experience in the transition zone, the committee recognized Kraig's potential and decided to hire him. Kraig began his tenure as the superintendent in February 2017 with high hopes for the future of the golf course and its greens.

As winter faded away and spring approached, the golf course and the greens emerged in excellent condition, showcasing a new beginning and generating excitement among the club members.

Kraig and his dedicated staff worked tirelessly to ensure that the greens would remain unparalleled throughout the summer, implementing their expertise and knowledge to maintain the pristine quality of our greens.

With the Men's Invitational Tournament on the horizon, anticipation grew as the greens were prepared to withstand the tournament's challenges. In the eyes of the players and spectators, the greens appeared to be in great condition, reflecting the hard work and dedication put forth by Kraig and his team. However, shortly after the tournament, unexpectedly, the greens began to turn brown, raising concerns among the club members.

Undeterred by this setback, Kraig remained resolute, insisting that there was nothing inherently wrong with the greens. Unfortunately, just two days later, the greens were completely dead, leaving the club members and staff perplexed and disappointed.

Critics and skeptics were quick to claim that maintaining bent greens in this particular area was impossible, despite the Country Club of Paducah continuing to maintain its greens with minimal issues. The problems that plagued the CC of Paducah in the late '80s and '90s were now a thing of the past, as they had successfully overcome those challenges. While they did experience minor problems with a few greens, they never encountered the same catastrophic issue experienced at our club.

Larry Hantle, the former longtime superintendent of CC of Paducah, had retired a few years earlier, and the new superintendent was achieving excellent results. This new superintendent had previously worked under Larry's guidance and came highly recommended by Larry, having accumulated valuable experience within the transition zone.

Chapter 26
FIN TRAGIQUE

Rolling Hills, being a prestigious country club with a rich history spanning six decades, faced its fair share of challenges over the years. However, the last 13 years have presented a particularly arduous journey. During this time, a decline in membership rocked the club's financial stability, posing a grave threat to its survival.

Adding to the woes, the club suffered the loss of its greens under the supervision of a new superintendent. This setback dealt a severe blow to membership numbers. By the close of 2017, the club, once bustling with activity, saw its membership plummet to a less than 300 regular members. Although there was a consensus among the board and the majority of members to revert the greens back to Bermuda – specifically, a resilient strain of dwarf Bermuda that could endure harsh winters with the aid of covers while still allowing year-round play – the club's dire financial state made securing funds for the project a daunting task.

The following year brought no relief, with no new members joining the ranks. By May, the club found itself grappling to meet its monthly expenses. It became increasingly clear that without a substantial injection of funds, the club's very existence hung in the balance. Concerned members convened to explore the option of acquiring the club. But, given the staggering debt and financial hurdles, it became evident that this pursuit would entail significant risks.

As the year progressed and the board exhausted all available options, the unfortunate decision to file for bankruptcy became inevitable. This marked yet another chapter in the storied history of the Lakeview property, which dates back to 1926 and signaled an imminent end. Looking back, if only the greens issue had been addressed earlier through the hiring of a superintendent skilled in maintaining bent greens, the inevitable decline in membership could have been averted.

Rolling Hills appeared to be on the brink of collapse as the bankruptcy proceedings unfolded. Remarkably, the club experienced a mild summer, and the greens fared relatively well with only a few minor issues. If this had been the norm for the past 13 years, our current predicament would most likely have been avoided. Unfortunately, that was not the case, and the end was rapidly approaching. As a result, the courts ordered an auction for the property, with a scheduled date of October 12, 2018.

As the auction date drew near, tension and skepticism permeated the atmosphere regarding the fate of the Rolling Hills property, particularly its prestigious golf and country club. Local groups with ample financial resources emerged, determined to preserve the property's rich heritage and maintain it as a thriving country club. They conducted detailed surveys among the current members to gauge their willingness to continue their cherished membership with a modest increase in dues. These discussions not only reflected their commitment to the club but also their deep connection to the vibrant community that had grown around it.

There were intriguing discussions about introducing a full-service restaurant for lunch and dinner to further enhance the club's offerings and attract a broader range of members. The idea was met with enthusiasm as it promised to create a delightful culinary experience and strengthen ties among the members. However, it was proposed that each member would be required to spend a minimum of $100 per month in the restaurant, contributing to its financial viability and sustainability.

Also, to ensure the long-term financial stability of the club, there were plans to adjust fees associated with golf-related services.

Cartshed rental for personal carts and yearly trail fees were likely to be revised to align with the industry standards and the club's ongoing operational costs. These adjustments aimed to strike a balance between providing excellent facilities and maintaining a sound financial footing for the club's future.

To attract potential buyers from across the nation, an auction company from Nashville, TN, was enlisted. Their expertise and reputation in handling high-profile auctions added a touch of prestige to the event, instilling confidence in both the sellers and potential buyers. Various investment groups, similar to the previous owners of the property, also expressed keen interest in acquiring the Rolling Hills property. Their intentions, however, remained shrouded in mystery, leaving the community eager to discover the future plans for this iconic establishment.

One unresolved matter that lingered throughout the auction preparations pertained to a commitment made by the original board to the members in 1985. It involved the sale of $300 certificates that were issued to raise funds for the down payment to purchase the property. These certificates were initially refundable upon leaving the club, provided the membership level remained at 500.

But, if the membership fell below 500, the certificates would be redeemed on a first-come basis once the membership reached 500 again. In 1988, recognizing the need to prevent further debt accumulation, the board approved a by-law change making the certificates non-redeemable for future members. This decision aimed to safeguard the club's financial stability while ensuring a fair distribution of any surplus funds to the loyal members who had supported the club during the challenging time of purchasing the property.

Regrettably, the club's recordkeeping for members who had resigned and had been among the original members purchasing the

$300 redeemable certificates between 1985 and the by-law change in 1988 was either nonexistent or misplaced, posing a challenge for the current officers. Despite their earnest efforts, they were unable to locate the necessary documentation to determine the exact number of former members eligible for potential reimbursement. In response, Judge Albert Reeder, presiding over the bankruptcy, ruled that former members who were part of the club during that period and were no longer active members would have a grace period of six months to provide evidence of their past membership. This decision had the purpose of fairness and transparency in distributing any surplus funds that might arise from the auction.

The much-anticipated auction took place in the elegant ballroom of Rolling Hills at precisely 2:05 PM, creating an atmosphere of exhilaration. Attendance was limited to a select group of 50 individuals, including authorized bidders and those fortunate enough to obtain exclusive tickets for observation. Only those in possession of a bidder's ticket or a spectator's ticket were granted access to the pristine grounds of Rolling Hills, heightening the exclusivity and allure of the event.

A total of 15 bidders, hailing from different corners of the country, had successfully met the stringent qualifications to participate. Each bidder was supported by financial letters from their respective banks, providing assurance of their capacity to fulfill their financial obligations and complete the transaction smoothly. The presence of these qualified bidders instilled confidence in the sellers and ensured the competitiveness of the auction.

The auctioneer, renowned for orchestrating successful sales of real estate properties, initiated the proceedings with an opening bid of $1,000,000. The bidding process quickly escalated as a local group promptly claimed the opening bid, signaling their ardent desire to acquire the prestigious Rolling Hills property. Shortly thereafter, another bid of $1.25 million emerged, followed swiftly by a bid surpassing $1.5 million. These initial bids, originating from different individuals, offered a glimmer of hope that the auction would prove successful in addressing the outstanding debts and expenses associated with the property's bankruptcy.

The room experienced a brief pause as bidders temporarily retreated for approximately five minutes, strategizing and recalibrating their bidding tactics. Suddenly, a bid of $2 million materialized, injecting renewed excitement into the auction and bringing the potential resolution of the club's debt closer at hand. Unexpectedly, a local group countered with a bid of $2.1 million, only to be swiftly surpassed at $2.3 million by a determined bidder. The auctioneer, well-versed in the art of orchestrating bidding wars, relished the unfolding scenario and skillfully facilitated the competitive spirit among the bidders.

Thirty minutes later, following an array of additional bids, the auction reached a remarkable milestone, with the amount rising to an impressive $3.2 million. Not only would this substantial sum successfully address the club's debt, but it would also yield a significant surplus to be distributed among the members, including former members with redeemable certificates. The auction room resonated with anticipation and excitement as the moment of truth approached.

Once again, a lull in bidding suggested the conclusion of the auction, prompting the auctioneer to commence the final countdown in a dramatic fashion: "Going once, going twice..." However, just as the atmosphere began to settle, a bid of $3.3 million emerged from a new bidder, an individual unfamiliar with the local area. This unexpected bid left everyone in suspense, pondering the intentions and vision this bidder might have for the beloved Rolling Hills property.

The attending members, who had closely followed the auction proceedings, once again grew concerned about the property's viability for a continued golf and country club under the new potential owner. As the bidding continued, three more bids were placed, gradually increasing the amount to an impressive $3.5 million. A hush fell over the room, and all eyes turned towards the auctioneer as the final countdown commenced: "Going once, going twice, SOLD!" The gavel struck the podium, marking the end of a transformative chapter for Rolling Hills.

With the conclusion of the auction, the fate of the Rolling Hills property was sealed, and a new era awaited. While the community eagerly awaited the reveal of the property's new owner, the successful auction not only ensured the resolution of the club's financial obligations, but all members, including those original ones, received an equal share of the surplus!

Chapter 27
LIFE GOES ON

Looking at the challenges faced by Rolling Hills Country Club, we are grateful that the ending differed from what was described in the previous chapter. The purpose of presenting it that way was to showcase just how close we came to the devastating demise of the club. In late April of 2018, our financial situation was precarious, particularly after losing our greens for the 9th time in 13 years. With declining membership resulting in reduced income from monthly dues, there was concern about securing financing for the conversion of our greens to Champions Bermuda.

While The Country Club of Paducah managed to maintain their bent greens with minimal issues, we were running out of time. Desperate measures were necessary to reassure our members, stem the exodus, and save the club. Fortunately, our board of directors exhibited strong leadership and quickly established contact with Champions Turf Farms from Bay City, TX. Within a short period, we obtained an estimate for the conversion to Champions G12 Bermuda grass for our greens.

After obtaining the figures, our leadership devised a plan that ultimately secured the required financing and facilitated the restructuring of our debt. In late June, we began the process of converting our greens, utilizing our in-house labor to prepare them for the sprigging of the Champions G12 Bermuda grass. The process unfolded smoothly, and by the fall of 2018, we were once again enjoying golf on our permanent greens. This time, the Bermuda grass-putting surface thrived and remained in excellent condition throughout the summer months. We are now optimistic. that our long nightmare is over. Thanks to covers installed during extreme temperatures below 32 degrees, we could play on our Dwarf Bermuda greens year-round.

One notable difference from bentgrass is the putting condition. While bent grass offers a consistent condition year-round, Dwarf Bermuda presents three distinct conditions throughout the year. During the summer, when the Bermuda grass thrives, the putting conditions are optimal. In spring and fall, when the grass is semi-dormant, the conditions are not perfect, but they are still acceptable. In winter, when the grass is dormant, putting becomes much more challenging. However, one thing is certain - we no longer lose our greens during the hot, humid summer months.

Fast forward to 2024, and Rolling Hills has not encountered any catastrophic issues as we had with bent greens, and memories of those challenges are fading. Our membership has rebounded, and our financial condition is in excellent shape. Over the past years, the golf course has seen significant improvements, thanks to a dedicated golf course committee and the hard work of our superintendents. Also, the costly burden of maintaining and re-seeding bent greens is over.

It is worth mentioning that the PGA TPC course in Memphis, TN, which hosts the annual professional tournament, FedEx St. Jude Championship, was initially constructed with bent grass greens. Even with the resources of the PGA, they faced problems with the greens and eventually converted to Champions Bermuda, which is still in use today.

Looking ahead, Rolling Hills Country Club is excited to continue providing an exceptional golfing experience to its members and guests. With the successful transition to Champions Bermuda greens, we can confidently say that our golf course is now better equipped to withstand the challenges of varying seasons and ensure a consistently enjoyable game for all.

APPENDIX

The following is the original layout of the 18 holes at Lakeview Country Club by architect Perry Maxwell.

Hole 1: 312 yard Par 4- Fairly straight hole with the green situated on a second hill. It requires a blind second shot into the elevated green. To the right of the fairway is a wooded area.

Hole 2: 307 yard Par 4- Another fairly straight hole. Driving over a deep ravine with an approach shot in trouble if it goes over the green where there is dense undergrowth of timber, giving an attractive backdrop for the green.

Hole 3: 540 yard Par 5- This is the longest hole on the course, with a fairway that slopes from right to left from tee to green. The drive is over a ditch 125 yards from the tee, landing short of a second-deep ditch. The second shot requires accuracy and proper length, and it is short of a third ditch to set up a short third shot. The green is guarded by the third ditch and well-placed sand traps with an attractive landscape behind and to the left.

Hole 4: 325 yard Par 4- The drive is over a large ditch and up a hill, presently a second shot with little difficulty.

Hole 5: 369 yard Par 4- This is a very difficult dogleg right with the drive to a hillside with a heavy slope. The second shot will be played from a hanging lie over a deep ravine to the green, which crowns a hill 150 yards away.

Hole 6: 153 yard Par 3- This hole is a fine test of either mashie or iron shot over a large ravine with timber growing on either side of the green. A tee shot on the green, which is on the crown of a gently rounded hill, should be able to handle par with ease. A missed or poorly played tee shot will make par nearly impossible.

Hole 7: 326 yard Par 4- This hole is the exact opposite of the fifth hole, with a drive to a hillside sloping heavily to the left. The second shot is to a green built on the opposite side of a deep ravine cut out of the hillside. A long drive and accurate approach shot will be needed to make par.

Hole 8: 196 yard Par 3- The tee is attractively located on the crown of a hill surrounded by trees with the green on an opposite hill. Requiring a wood or long iron to reach the putting surface and the undulation of the green adds to the difficulty of the hole.

Hole 9: 420 yard Par 4- This hole is challenging to even the most accomplished golfer. It is a dogleg right with the fairway being bordered by heavy timber on both sides. The green is a perfect golf picture, located on a naturally sloping shelf and surrounded on three sides by trees. It is located back at the clubhouse, allowing players who desire to play only nine holes to end their match near home.

Hole 10: 417 yard Par 4- The tee is to the immediate right of the clubhouse and requires a drive over a yawning chasm to reach the fairway on the opposite hillside. The fairway borders the northern shore of the lake and is both difficult and beautiful. A good drive leaves a long, straight-second shot to reach the green that is carved out of a steep hillside. A large ditch in front of the green will catch a poor shot. This hole will prove to be one of the hardest holes on the course.

Hole 11: 409 yard Par 4- A long straight drive leaves a relatively simple shot to the green, which is placed in an attractive setting of trees, small growth, and a deep ditch short of the green. The hole goes around the western dam at the end of the lake.

Hole 12: 391 yard Par 4- Another difficult hole, calling for a long straight uphill drive and a long second shot to a green set in primeval timber. Trees border both sides of the latter half of the fairway, with the hole following the southern shore of the lake.

Hole 13: 324 yard Par 4- A relatively easy hole with a drive from a tee on the crown of one hill to a fairway that crowns another with a deep ditch between. The green is guarded by woods and a ditch.

Hole 14: 178 yard Par 3- The distance would indicate a midiron, but with the green elevated a substantial amount above the tee on a steep hillside, most players will have to use a spoon or brassie.

Hole 15: 436 yard Par 4- This is one of the extremely difficult holes on the Lakeview course and became Mr. Maxwell's favorite. The entire hole from tee to green is bordered with heavy timber, with a tee that looks out from the edge of a steep bluff to a narrow winding fairway. A good drive gives the player a full view of the distant green located on the brow of a steep hill, many feet higher than the fairway.

Hole 16: 399 yard Par 4- Another hard hole calling for a drive over a ravine with a ditch at the bottom to a crown of a hill 200 years away. The green slopes with the hillside are well guarded by small trees on one side and a well-placed sand trap on the other side.

Hole 17: 135 yard Par 3- The mashie niblick or the mashie shot to this long, narrow, closely guarded green must be accurate, or par will be challenging. The tee is on the brow of a sloping hill with the green across a little valley and cut out of the side of the opposite hill.

Hole 18: 524 yard Par 5- This is the most difficult right-angle dogleg. The drive is over a deep ditch immediately in front of the tee and up a long, slanting hill. The second shot is down a tree-bordered fairway to within 75 yards of a beautifully elevated natural sloping green surrounded by trees.

Milton Keynes UK
Ingram Content Group UK Ltd.
UKHW050923121124
450964UK00007B/74